1942

THE ROMAN USE OF ANECDOTES
IN
CICERO, LIVY, AND THE SATIRISTS

THE ROMAN USE OF ANECDOTES IN CICERO LIVY, & THE SATIRISTS

BY

ELIZABETH HAZELTON HAIGHT

Professor of Latin, Vassar College

NEW YORK

LONGMANS, GREEN AND CO.

M D CCCC XL

Published in Celebration of
the Seventy-Fifth Anniversary
of
VASSAR COLLEGE
and
in honor of
HENRY NOBLE MacCRACKEN
in the twenty-fifth year
of his Presidency

The Publication

of this book was made possible

by the

J. LEVERETT MOORE RESEARCH FUND

IN CLASSICS

and the

LUCY MAYNARD SALMON FUND

FOR RESEARCH

established at Vassar College

in 1926

PREFACE

BEFORE I can hope to have my publishers set a *feliciter explicit* on this book, I must conclude, by a sort of hysteron-proteron, with a foreword of explanation and thanks. "The Roman Use of Anecdotes," Gentle Reader, is not a trivial subject, however slight it may seem. The Romans saw such aesthetic and moral possibilities in the small story that the composition of it was a serious part of their education. They used the anecdote not only to enliven their literature but to convey great truths. So my book is a study of a literary form which is more important than the gem, the statuette, or the miniature in art. In its small compass you may see the speaking likenesses of many persons of many times, their manners and their morals. I challenge your interest with a paraphrase of Martial :

> He misses what an anecdote may say
> Who thinks it voices merely jests and play.

Special thanks are due to the President and Fellows of Harvard College for permission to quote freely the translations of *The Loeb Classical Library,* and to E. P. Dutton and Co. for permission to use a version of Martial from the *Broadway Translations.* Professor J. Wight Duff of the University of Durham, Dean Paul Nixon of Bowdoin College, and Professor Gilbert Highet of Columbia University have all graciously allowed me to quote material from their writings. Professor Maud W. Makemson,

Chairman of the Department of Astronomy of Vassar College, kindly verified for me the lunar eclipse of 168 B.C. My appreciation is due also to those faculty colleagues in two research clubs, the Classical Journal Club and Pot Luck, who listened to various chapters of my book and encouraged me by their interest.

I am happy in having a volume to contribute to a series in honor of the Seventy-Fifth Anniversary of Vassar College, in whose *reducta valle* I received an inspiring education, found satisfying work, and have made my home.

> Alme Sol, curru nitido diem qui
> promis et celas aliusque et idem
> nasceris, possis nihil VASSAR COLLEGE
>   visere maius.

And to Henry Noble MacCracken, the scholar-president, *docte sermones utriusque linguae,* who has given me understanding sympathy for my teaching and writing, I offer another Roman wish :

> *macte virtute esto !*

CONTENTS

THE ROMAN USE OF ANECDOTES
in Cicero, Livy, and the Satirists

I

THE ART OF WRITING ANECDOTES

THE Romans had such a gift for telling little stories that the very title, "The Art of Writing Anecdotes," recalls to memory certain famous anecdotes in Latin authors : Damocles at the tyrant's banquet under the hair-suspended sword, old Sophocles on trial for his sanity reading to his judges his new play "Oedipus at Colonus," the fable of the country mouse and the city mouse, the satire of the chaste woman of Ephesus.   The assemblage of Latin anecdotes is legion, their art is a truism.

Nevertheless before we begin to study the technique of this neglected, miniature art form in its use in special authors, we must face the rather onerous task of seeing what the theorists thought of the use of anecdotes.   We must discover whether the writing of them played any part in Roman education.   And we must consider what the relation of the anecdote was to the longer narration which formed so vital a division of Roman oratory and which was one of the precursors of the Latin novel.

Our sources for any such study will naturally be the rhetorical writings of the *Auctor ad Herennium,* of Cicero, Seneca the Elder, Quintilian.   And a special debt to secondary sources must be mentioned, for Paul Lejay in his preface to his edition of the Satires of Horace and George Converse Fiske in his "Lucilius and Horace" *inter alios* have paved an open road to such investigation.

What is an anecdote ?   That is the first question to
raise.   The Oxford English Dictionary defines the word
as true to its Greek origin at first (from ἀνέκδοτα, things un-
published) meaning "secret, private, or hitherto unpub-
lished narratives or details of history," but then shifting
from this idea of "an item of gossip" to "the narrative of
a detached incident or of a single event, told as being in
itself interesting or striking."   Probably this is what the
word anecdote means to most of us today.   However before we can study the anecdotes of Latin writers with
success, we must go back to Latin definitions of the anecdote and to ancient classifications of different types of it.
So too the technical terms used by the ancient critics in
their discussions must be clarified.   And from the outset
we must fix in our minds the fact that in ancient discussions of literary style and the technique of writing no distinction was made between poetry and prose.   Cicero's
characterizations of the grand style and the plain style in
oratory correspond closely with Horace's distinction between different types of poetry.[1]   Cicero's perfect or ideal
orator is matched by Horace's true poet.   Cicero's theory
of the use of anecdotes could be illustrated as well from
the Latin satirists as from Cicero's orations.

A study of the terms used for anecdotes and their
definitions shows that Latin writers inherited from the
Cynic philosophy certain definite literary forms with their
styles.   These are the diatribe, the χρεία (in Latin the exemplum), the apophthegm; and to these must be added
for clearness of classification the testimonium and the
fable or apologue.

The diatribe which was a pedantic successor of the
dialogue was a discussion in the form of a monologue de-

[1] Compare Inez G. Scott, "The Grand Style in the Satires of Juvenal," Smith
College Classical Studies, Northampton, 1927, pp. 7-13.

livered by a teacher to a pupil. Its tone remained that
of the dialogue, simple, informal. As it was a speech, it
owed its literary form in origin to the stenographer or to
a report made from memory. The homily, ὁμιλία, was a
subdivision of the diatribe, a speech designed for all the
people, not addressed to one individual.[2]

The χρεία is very different from the diatribe. It is defined clearly by Charisius : Chria est dicti vel facti prae-
cipua memoratio.[3] "The *chria* is a clear account of
something that has been said or something that has been
done." Charisius gives sufficient illustrations of the *chria*
to expand his definition. On the basis of his account Lejay [4] interprets the *chria* as a significant fact, a piquant or
sententious saying. It differs from the maxim, γνώμη, in
that it is related to a particular event or person. It is intel-
lectual or witty. It is used in a narrative which explains
it. It may be a short narrative arranged to lead up to a
point of view or to an action at the end. Of this type
Horace's Satires I. 7 and 8 are good illustrations.

The *chria* as its name shows had originally a utilitarian
object, and for this reason it owed its origin to the more
practical schools of Greek philosophy, the Cynic and the
Stoic, nevertheless it did not belong exclusively to these
schools. Aristippus, the Cyrenaic, wrote three books of
chriae.[5] These anecdotes were used apparently in meetings of philosophers of different schools, for the examples
given by Charisius show Antisthenes opposed to Aristippus, Aristotle to Diogenes. Collections of *chriae* were
made by pupils of the great teachers in these schools, by
Metrocles, the disciple of Crates, by Persaeus, the disciple
of Zeno. The *chriae* gradually passed from the schools
of the philosophers to those of the grammaticus and of the

[2] P. Lejay, *Œuvres d'Horace, Satires*, Paris, 1911, p. XV.
[3] Keil, *Gram. Lat.* 6, p. 273.
[4] Lejay, *op. cit.*, pp. XVII–XIX.
[5] Diogenes Laertius, II. 84, 85.

rhetor.   The *chria* is identical with the *exemplum* whose use was taught in these Roman schools.[6]

The *exemplum* is carefully defined in the *Auctor ad Herennium*,[7] as "a setting forth of some action or saying of the past attached to the name of a particular authority." Its functions are to embellish subject matter, or to clarify it, or to make it more probable. "It places its subject before the eyes since it describes everything so clearly that I would say it can almost be touched by the hand." Quintilian adds to this definition the fact that the subject matter of the anecdote may be fictitious as well as historical and he emphasizes one object in the use of *exempla,* that of persuading an audience of the point of view of the orator.[8]

The *testimonium* was distinguished from the *exemplum* by the rhetoricians.   Cicero says that everything which is introduced from a foreign source to produce belief is called *testimonium.*[9]   It may be then a mere quotation, but the words are usually those of distinguished men : statesmen, orators, philosophers, or of literary men, poets, historians.   It may even be a general truth, a proverb, an oracle, a text of law.   The *exemplum* can never be a mere quotation, but *exemplum* and *testimonium* have one great field in common, the apophthegm or maxim.

The apophthegm was the delight of the Romans.   Cato the Elder at the end of his life made a collection of the apophthegms of Socrates.   Collections of such sayings were made by both Cicero and Julius Caesar.   Melissus, the freedman of Maecenas and the librarian of the Porticus of Octavia, wrote one hundred and fifty books of max-

---

[6] For this summary see Lejay, *op. cit.,* pp. xix–xxii and G. C. Fiske, *Lucilius and Horace,* Madison, 1920, pp. 159–62.

[7] IV, 49, 62.

[8] Quintilian, *Institutio Oratoria,* V. xi, 6.

[9] Cic. *Topica,* 73, 78.

ims called *Ineptiae.* The Apophthegms of Plutarch give some idea of these lost collections. The form was adopted by Christianity and appeared in the sayings of the Fathers of the Desert and the *Florilegia.* Apophthegms were revived in a philosophic type in the Renaissance in the Adages of Erasmus.

Lejay after this history of the Apophthegm proceeds to explain why to his mind the *chria* or *exemplum* had such popularity among the Romans. The Roman had a taste for the particular, for the individual. In history he was more interested in the small fact, the curious detail, the trait of character than in the developments of politics or war. Valerius Maximus would appeal to a larger number of readers than would Polybius. Titus Livius is a sort of superior Valerius Maximus who found the unity of history in the greatness of Rome, but who treated Rome almost like a person. His epitomists retain the anecdotes and the remarkable speeches. Horace responded to this national taste in sowing his Satires with anecdotes.[10] These are Lejay's comments.

One special class of anecdotes must be defined before we begin the detailed study of the *exemplum,* that is, the fable. The αἶνος or fable is a name applied first to a story in which animals or inanimate objects like trees talk. Later on in the history of the fable the beasts develop a moral sense and preach so that the fable becomes a kind of moral tale. The true fable deals with beasts or inanimate objects, the Apologue or Moral Tale with human beings.[11] Fables as they arose in folk lore and then came to be the property of many a story-teller finally took traditional form and were associated with one great name, that of Aesop. Quintilian [12] comments on the pleasure

10 Lejay, *op. cit.,* p. xxi.   12 Quintilian, *I. O.,* V. xi, 19.
11 J. A. K. Thomson, *The Art of the Logos,* London, 1935, pp. 19, 65-73.

they give to simple, uneducated people and on the fact that they formed effective arguments for the *plebs*. So Menenius Agrippa is said to have won the people back to harmony with the patricians by his fable of the human body in which it is impossible for the limbs to revolt against the belly. This form of anecdote will have a special chapter of its own in a study of the Latin fabulist, Phaedrus.

Before, however, we turn to the use of anecdotes in certain authors, in Cicero, in Livy, in the satirists, in Phaedrus and Martial, we must read what Fiske calls "the testimony of Seneca and Quintilian" that the χρεία played an important part in the education of the young.[13] Cicero referred to *exempla* as the most effective embellishments of the style of an oration, really *lumina* for its illumination.[14]   And in his magnificent description of the art of the ideal orator he mentions among the *ornamenta* of an oration the use of anecdotes.[15]   Seneca urges that in the schools such *exempla* should be memorized by boys because their young minds receive them with pleasure and from them they learn wisdom.[16]   Quintilian gives more specific directions about instruction on the writing of anecdotes in the schools of the grammaticus.[17] Pupils should be taught to relate Aesop's fables in simple language in the plain style. Then they should be given practice in writing maxims and *exempla*. The themes of the *exempla* may be either deeds or sayings. Quintilian offers two pertinent illustrations of themes which teachers might set :
"Crates, when he had seen a badly educated boy, flogged his pedagogue" ; "Milo, who had accustomed himself to carrying a calf every day, carried it when it was a bull." In another passage Quintilian states that the *exempla* are

13 G. C. Fiske, *op. cit.*, p. 160.
14 Cic. *de Orat.* III. lii, 201.
15 Cic. *Orator.* XL, 137-38.
16 Seneca, *Ep.* 33.
17 Quintilian, *I. O.*, I. ix, 2-6.

vital tools, not of the art of the orator, but of the orator
himself ; he must therefore have a rich supply of anecdotes in his mind : real ones drawn from history and contemporary life, fictitious ones from the great poets ; these
are the tools of knowledge and experience ready to shape
moral lessons for his hearers.[18]   From all these passages
it is clear that part of the training in the Roman schools
which Livy, Horace, Persius, Juvenal, Martial must have
received was practice in writing *exempla* under the direction of their teachers, and that these were to be used
as ornaments of style, or to teach morals, or to persuade
the minds of hearers.

In another place, I tried to show how in the rhetorical
schools the preparation and delivery of *suasoriae* and *controversiae* gave training in the art of writing fiction.[19]
Now a third form of imaginative writing which was part
of the training of the orator, that is of all young men who
attended the schools of the rhetors, must be considered.
That is, the part of an oration which was called the *narratio*.

At the risk of carrying owls to Athens I must mention
here the well-known divisions of an oration and state the
characteristics of the *narratio* as outlined in the *Auctor
ad Herennium*.   There are six parts of a speech : the
exordium, the beginning of a speech by which the mind
of the hearer is aroused to listen ; the *narratio,* the setting
forth of facts or fiction ; the *divisio,* the outline of the
subject under discussion and the points to be taken up ;
the *confirmatio,* the statement of arguments with proof ;
the *confutatio,* the overthrow of the opponent's arguments ; the *conclusio,* the carefully worked out peroration.

"*Narratio* is of three kinds : (*a*) the statement of the

18 Quintilian, *I. O.,* XII. iv, 1-2.
19 E. H. Haight, *Essays on Ancient Fiction,* New York, 1936, pp. 121-50.

case ; (b) narrations introduced to gain credit, to disparage
the opponent, and for similar purposes ; (c) illustrative
narratives, either mythological, historical or fictitious." [20]
In style the *narratio* demands three essential qualities :
brevity, clarity, plausibility.[21]   The language for the sake
of clarity must be simple and colloquial.   And finally
here as in the whole oration it is the handling of the facts
that commands admiration.[22]

From these strictures about the *narratio* it is easy to see
that it is closely related to the *exemplum*.   It too is the
telling of a story.   It too must be brief, clear and per-
suasive.   Both are lights or ornaments.   Indeed the narrative part of a speech seems almost a magnified or ex-
panded anecdote.   Certainly both demand the same qualities of narrative art.   This fact appears most clearly
when, in the *narratio, exempla* are used, stories within
stories, told with the same conciseness and persuasiveness
which characterize the longer narrative, all calculated to
play upon the thought or emotions of the hearer and so
to convince his opinion or move his feeling to action.

Perhaps a chief reason why the Romans were such good
story-tellers was that in their education, the climax of
which was training in oratory, the audience always had to
be in the mind of the speaker or writer.   The functions
of oratory were to prove statements (that is to instruct),
to persuade and to move men.   Cicero says that what is
true of the parts of an oration must be true of the whole.[23]
And conversely the standards of the whole speech must
apply to the parts.   Hence the *narratio* as well as the
whole oration must always think of the audience.   So too
must the *exemplum,* the miniature *narratio,* in whatever

[20] *Auctor ad Herennium,* I. 3, 8–9,
summarized by A. S. Wilkins in *de
Oratore,* pp. 53–54.

[21] See also Cic. *de Orat.* II. 80–81,
264.
[22] Cic. *Orator,* 124.
[23] Cic. *de Orat.* II. 80–81, 83.

kind of writing it is employed. Therefore because a story, short or long, must always be told with a view to its effect on its auditors, its essential characteristics must be such brevity or selection of material that nothing can be subtracted from its finished form, such clarity that its meaning is obvious to the average listener, such probability that no attack can be made on preposterous assumptions in it, such simplicity of style that one man shall seem to be talking to another in the language of every day, and finally such vividness that objects and persons described shall seem present, represented to the eye, yes, even to the touch so that visibility and tangibility are achieved through mere words. It is this art of which the Romans were supreme masters.

The use of the anecdote in certain Latin writers may now be studied. Cicero's technique in handling it will be considered first because he affords the best Latin illustration of the work of both critic and artist in the field of narration. Moreover the range of his writings gives opportunity to observe how he varied his use of anecdotes in oratory, essays, and dialogues. Next Livy will be studied as the master of the art of narration in the writing of history. Then since the satirists found in the anecdotes one of their most effective tools, we shall consider the art of the anecdote in Horace, Phaedrus, Martial, Persius and Juvenal.

II

CICERO'S ART OF NARRATION

Cicero in his rhetorical writings makes the orator's three functions to teach, to delight, to persuade, *docere, delectare, flectere*.   These he must exercise by a sure mastery of three different styles of speech, the grand, the intermediate, the plain, and by a skillful employment of them and of the figures which are the ornaments of oratory, the *lumina verborum et sententiarum.* Throughout each speech, the orator must have his mind on his audience and consider what the ancients called ἦθος and πάθος in his relation to his hearers.   The idea of ἦθος includes all that bears on man's character and conduct as a member of a social group and 'man' here must refer to both speaker and hearer.   Πάθος embraces all the emotion aroused in the audience by the speaker.[1]   It is important to remember all these generalizations about the ideal orator because Cicero's theory illumines his technique in every part of his writing, even in his anecdotes.

From the vast storehouse of Cicero's works, from the variety of types of literature employed by him (letters, orations, dialogues, rhetorical and philosophical treatises) I have selected illustrations which seem to show the art of his narration from the simplest anecdote of a few lines to the long stories which might be called *novelle* and were indeed written as fiction.

[1] Cic. *Orator* and *de Oratore, passim.*

The Dialogue in which Cato, Scipio and Laelius discuss old age is rich in small anecdotes, introduced naturally in conversation to illustrate some point for the speaker. They turn, as the definition of the *exemplum* would lead us to expect, on some saying or on some action. Cato when he wishes to prove that old age may be calm and peaceful recalls a remark of Gorgias the sophist who lived one hundred and seven years, and never abated his zeal and labor. When someone inquired of him why he wished to live so long, he replied : "I have no accusation to bring against old age." [2] Again when Cato is meeting the charge that old age has lost all pleasures of the senses, he relates how the aged Sophocles on being asked whether he enjoyed the pleasures of love, exclaimed : "Heaven help me ! I have gladly escaped from them as from a mad and boorish slave-master." [3] These are typical anecdotes of famous sayings by great men.

Told with the same brevity and conciseness are other small stories of actions. One of the most famous illustrates the saying "old men retain their wits," *manent ingenia senibus,* and is likewise of Sophocles.[4]

Sophocles wrote tragedies to the very end of his long life. On account of this zeal for writing he seemed to be neglecting his business affairs so his sons summoned him to court in order that a jury might pronounce him incompetent to manage his estate on the ground of senility. (Such provision the laws allow.) Then the old man is said to have recited to his judges a play which he had just finished and had in his hands, the *Oedipus at Colonus,* and to have asked whether the poem seemed the work of a man in his dotage. After his recitation he was freed by the vote of the jurors.

Now this anecdote was pregnant with meaning for Cato's hearers as he knew it would be, for they were

[2] Cic. *de Sen.* 13.   [4] Cic. *de Sen.* 22.
[3] Cic. *de Sen.* 47, Plato, *Rep.* I, 329 C.

familiar with the *Oedipus at Colonus,* the greatest play
ever written on old age, in which the dethroned, blind,
unhappy monarch finds at last peace and mystic death at
the nightingale-haunted hill of the Kindly Goddesses.
The story therefore, simply and briefly told as it is, stirs
deep and spiritual memories of an old age triumphant
over ruin, exile, even death.

In contrast to this anecdote enriched by connotation
and association with tragedy and Athens, is a realistic portrayal of a Roman episode.   Cato is proving that one
blessing conferred by old age is the end of lust.   And to
illustrate what *libido* makes a man do he tells the event
which made him in his censorship expel Lucius Flamininus from the senate.   Flamininus, when as consul he was
in Gaul, was persuaded at a banquet by a harlot to have
a condemned prisoner beheaded with an axe.[5]   Here an
historical fact whose horror speaks for itself is mentioned
to arouse indignation against ruinous lust which entails
personal disgrace and public dishonor.

These four illustrations are typical of Cicero's use of
anecdotes in the Dialogue on Old Age.   Most of them are
drawn from Greek sources.   They record sayings or actions of famous persons.   They are brief, concise, pointed.
They enrich the dialogue though they are introduced in-
formally in natural conversation.   They not only adorn
it, but illuminate it.

Another work by Cicero which is rich in *exempla* is the
Tusculan Disputations.   This like the *de Senectute* is in
dialogue form, but is much longer for its five books represent discussions which took place on five successive days
at Cicero's Villa at Tusculum.   Here in the year 45 B.C.,
a group of young men who were staying with Cicero

[5] Cic. *de Sen.* 42.   Compare Livy, 39, 42.

listened to their master talk in the morning on rhetorical theory, in the afternoon on philosophy. Cicero says that in the true old Socratic way he called on his friends to propose subjects for discussion, listened to their views, then presented his own. His discourse, he says, is really a *declamatio,* one of the practice speeches taught in the Roman schools.[6] He admits that in these discourses he is presenting to his friends the thought of Greek philosophers, but he declares that he has followed his rule of not being bound by the tenets of any one school, rather of seeking the most probable solution of each problem.

The main thesis which Cicero presents in the *Tusculan Disputations* is this : philosophy shows that virtue may make men happy in spite of death, pain, and the distress and disorders of the soul. The object of Cicero's talks is clearly instruction, *docere.* Since this instruction is being given to a group of young men interested in rhetoric and philosophy, Cicero with his eyes always on his audience enlivens and illuminates his discourse by many anecdotes. Their sources are Greek. They are records of famous sayings and deeds. They have accumulative force, for often they are assembled in series, one illustration heaped upon another. Most of them have a philosophical point because of the subjects under discussion.

To illustrate the truth that no philosopher fears poverty, Cicero presents in quick succession illustrations from many schools : Epicurus, the Scythian Anacharsis, Socrates, Xenocrates, Diogenes the Cynic. Sayings of the last three are quoted for their pungent points. Socrates when he saw masses of gold and silver being carried along in a procession, exclaimed : "How many things there are I do not want !" Xenocrates when messengers from Al-

6 Cic. *Tusc. Dis.,* I. 7–8 ; II. 9 ; IV. 7.

exander brought him a large gift of fifty talents, entertained them with a simple supper at the Academy and when next day they asked him to whom they should deliver Alexander's gift, inquired : "What ?   Did you not perceive from last night's little supper that I have no need of money ?" Diogenes was even more outspoken. When Alexander asked him to name any need he had, the Cynic replied : "Now please move a little out of my sun." [7]

A similar series of anecdotes illustrates the proverb that hunger is the best sauce.   Darius in his flight from Alexander gladly drank muddy water polluted by corpses. Ptolemy, lost in Egypt, enjoyed poor bread in a country cottage.   Socrates used to walk until evening in order as he said that he might better enjoy his dinner.   When Dionysius could not stomach the black broth of the Spartans, the cook informed the tyrant that he had not the proper seasoning : "The hard work of hunting, sweat, a run to the Eurotas, hunger, thirst, by these things the dinners of the Lacedaemonians are seasoned." [8]   Variety is given to these anecdotes by having Socrates demonstrate in his everyday habits what potentates learned in crises and by having a great tyrant given instruction by a cook.

In another series, on death, each anecdote has a single point.   Death is not an evil : it may even be welcomed. How debonair Theramenes was when he was condemned to death by the Thirty Tyrants !   In his prison he drank the poison like a thirsty man, then tossed what was left out of the cup so it should make a splash as in a game and with a laugh gave a toast to the leader of his enemies : "I drink," said he, "to handsome Critias."   That remarkable man joked with his last breath and proposed the toast which was destined to be fatal to the Tyrant who killed

[7] Cic. *Tusc. Dis.* V. 91–92.   [8] Cic. *Tusc. Dis.* V. 97–98.

him. Cicero cannot refrain from personal comment on this episode : "How Theramenes delights me ! How gallant was his spirit !" [9]

Another group of *exempla* follows to prove that death may be despised not only by distinguished men but by whole armies, not only by men but by women. These illustrations, taken from the life of the Spartans, are pointed by famous quotations : the epitaph of the Lacedaemonians who fell at Thermopylae ; the remark of one Spartan who, when told before a battle that in it he would not see the sun for the number of the Persian javelins and arrows, remarked simply : "Then we shall fight in the shade !" ; the Spartan mother's comment on the death of her son in battle : "For this I bore him that he might be a man who would not hesitate to die for his country." [10] These are what I might call connotative or allusive anecdotes, relying for their poignancy on the auditors' knowledge of history and tradition.

Told at greater length is the famous story of Cleobis and Biton, sons of the priestess of Argos. There was a sacred festival to which the priestess by religious custom had to be drawn in a chariot. The precinct was far from the town, the oxen were slow. So the young men Cleobis and Biton took off their robes, rubbed their bodies with oil, took the place of the oxen at the yoke and drew their mother to the shrine. The priestess then prayed that for their devotion the goddess should give her sons the greatest boon a god could confer. The young men after dining with their mother went to sleep. In the morning they were found dead. So is death regarded by the gods. The simplicity of the telling of this story, its religious aura, make death seem indeed sleep's twin-brother which god giveth to his beloved.[11]

9 Cic. *Tusc. Dis.* I. 96–97.   11 Cic. *Tusc. Dis.* I. 113–14.
10 Cic. *Tusc. Dis.* I. 100–102.

Sometimes anecdotes are set in pairs that their significance may be intensified by the contrast of opposites. So to point the moral that pain is not an evil, first a story is told of Dionysius of Heraclea who, when attacked with kidney trouble, renounced the instruction of Zeno and admitted pain was an evil.   Then a story following shows how a philosopher conquered just as severe pain.   The hero is the Syrian Stoic, Posidonius.   It is a story which Pompey the Great liked to tell.   When he was traveling back from Syria to Italy, Pompey stopped at Rhodes.   He was eager to hear Posidonius lecture.   When he learned that Posidonius was very ill with arthritis, all the same he wished to call on the famous philosopher.   When Pompey had seen him and offered his homage and compliments, he said that he regretted deeply that he could not hear him.   But Posidonius said : "But you can.   I will not permit that pain of body should make so great a hero come to me in vain."   Then lying in bed Posidonius spoke with dignity and eloquence on the thesis that nothing is good except what is honorable, and when the fires of pain attacked him, he often exclaimed : "You accomplish nothing, Pain !   However troublesome you are, I will never admit that you are an evil." [12]   Here the anecdote is dramatized by a second narrator, since we see the Stoic's triumph over pain through the eyes not of a philosopher, but of a military conqueror.

Perhaps the most famous anecdote in the *Tusculans* is that of the sword of Damocles.   It is the climax of a series of anecdotes about Dionysius of Syracuse.   Together they paint a character sketch of the tyrant.   They are followed by a brief characterization of Archimedes, the scientist, introduced for contrast.

Dionysius was tyrant of Syracuse for thirty-eight years,

[12] Cic. *Tusc. Dis.* II. 61.

but his power gave him no happiness. That city of great beauty he held oppressed with slaves. And in spite of his moderate way of living, his energy and industry in affairs, he was by nature wicked and unjust. In spite of good family, high position, friends, lovers, he never attained his heart's desire even when he thought he was omnipotent. For he trusted no one and his life was dominated by fear.

He had no intimates but shut himself up as it were in a prison surrounded by guards of freedmen and barbarians. He would never trust his neck to a barber, but had his young daughters taught to shave him. When they were older, he did not trust even them with a razor, but had them singe off his hair and beard. He had two wives but visited them at night after the most careful inspection. Indeed he had a wide fosse built around his bed-room to be crossed only by a wooden drawbridge. This he himself let down and raised again before he closed the door of his bed-chamber. When he harangued the people, he spoke to them from a high tower. Once when he wished to play ball, his favorite sport, and laid aside his tunic, he is said to have handed his sword to a young man whom he loved. At this a certain acquaintance remarked in jest : "To this man certainly you entrust your life," and the youth with the sword smiled. Dionysius had them both put to death, one for indicating a way to murder him, the other for smiling at it. Nothing in his life caused him more grief than this execution, for he had loved passionately the young man whom he killed.

Dionysius realized fully that he was not happy. Indeed he demonstrated his inner life to a flattering courtier who on praising his wealth had called him most blessed of men. "Do you wish then, Damocles," he said, "since this my life pleases you, to savor it and try my fortune ?"

When Damocles said he did, he was placed on a magnificent couch at a Lucullan banquet with beautiful slaveboys at his beck and call.   There were perfumes, garlands, incense, exquisite food.   But suddenly Dionysius had let down from the ceiling a sword suspended by a horsehair so that it hung directly over the neck of the happy man.   Then Damocles could think of nothing else and soon he begged the tyrant to let him depart, for now he did not wish to be happy.

This was the state of mind of Dionysius in his self-isolation.   Here was an educated man who was a musician, a tragic poet (how good does not matter !) who did not enjoy the arts and the intercourse of human life.   He lived with slaves, criminals, barbarians.   He thought no man who was worthy of freedom or wished to be free, his friend.[13]

I have paraphrased at length Cicero's account of Dionysius because it shows well his use of ἦθος, or character-drawing, in its detailed anecdotes of the tyrant's daily life and in its revelation of his inner state of mind.   In its completeness it is an effective argument for the philosopher's point of view of the worthlessness of power.

The *Tusculan Disputations* were dedicated to Brutus. A year later when he became the Liberator and risked all, even his life, for the freedom of his country, perhaps he had in mind Cicero's picture of the tyrant who could not tolerate freedom in any man.   Then Cicero's function in this work, the instruction of young men, would have been broadened from *docere* to *flectere,* from influencing thought to stimulating action.   And his anecdotes would have served not only as *lumina* and *ornamenta,* but as *exempla* in the fullest sense of that word.

The third work which I have chosen to illustrate Cic-

13 Cic. *Tusc. Disc.* V. 57–63.

ero's use of anecdotes is the *de Officiis*. It was written in 44 B.C., after the death of Julius Caesar. It was addressed to Cicero's son, Marcus, then twenty-one years old, who was studying in Athens at the Peripatetic School of Cratippus. Its subject is propriety of conduct or moral duties. Its chief source is a treatise by Panaetius. In form it is not a dialogue, but a direct address to his son. It is therefore a prose forerunner of Horace's philosophical Epistles. It is the richest storehouse of anecdotes of all Cicero's writing. The stories are drawn from mythology, history, philosophy, business life. The object of the whole essay is to instruct, perhaps also to move young Cicero to a wiser conduct of his own life than he had so far achieved. The many anecdotes are clearly employed to attract a young man's attention and rivet his interest.

There are not many mythological anecdotes and these are familiar Greek stories. A series of three, each with the same point, illustrates the thesis that promises ought not to be kept when they are not useful to the very men to whom they were made. The sun god kept his promise to Phaethon that he would grant whatever he wished, so his son soared in his father's chariot to his death. Neptune fulfilled his promise to Theseus to grant him three wishes, and caused the death of his son Hippolytus. Agamemnon vowed to Diana the most beautiful creature born in his country in one year, so had to sacrifice his own daughter, Iphigenia. Promises which involve such disasters should be broken.[14]

Many historical anecdotes are used and these are largely Roman. "There are many famous illustrations [says Cicero] of times when a state has despised expedient action for the sake of its honor. Our country is rich in

[14] Cic. *de Off.* III. 94.

examples of many periods, and especially in the Second
Punic War.   After the news of the defeat at Cannae was
reported the Romans showed greater courage than in success : there was no sign of fear, no mention of peace."

Then Cicero elaborates this point by two examples
from Greek history.   In the Persian Wars when the
Athenians could not halt the invasion of the Persians,
they decided to abandon their city, transfer their wives
and children to Troezen, and defend the freedom of
Greece by their fleet.   When a certain Cyrsilus proposed
instead that they remain in Athens and receive Xerxes in
the city, they stoned him to death.

After the victory over the Persians, Themistocles announced to the Assembly that he had a plan for the public
safety which must be kept secret and he asked that the
Assembly should appoint a representative to discuss it
with him.   They selected Aristides.   Themistocles confided to him that the fleet of the Spartans which had
been beached near Gytheum could be secretly set on fire
and by the burning of it Sparta's power would be crushed.
Aristides reported back to the Assembly that Themistocles' plan was expedient, but not honorable.   It was
therefore rejected.[15]

A Roman series gives striking examples of the part good
faith played in Roman honor.   A promise given by an
individual to an enemy must be kept. Regulus kept faith
with the Carthaginians when he did not effect the exchange of prisoners for which he was sent to Rome, when
indeed he advised against the measure, for he returned
voluntarily to death in a Carthaginian prison to keep his
word.   This story is retold in Book III, with a long ethical discussion of the nobility and heroism of his conduct.
Detractors who criticized his action are answered on the

[15] Cic. *de Off.* III. 47-49.

ground that he acted in accordance with Roman principles of justice and good faith.[16]

When Hannibal after the battle of Cannae sent ten Roman captives to Rome to secure an exchange of prisoners and they did not succeed in this but remained in Rome, the censors kept them disfranchised for life because they had broken faith.

Justice toward an enemy was shown by the Romans in the war with Pyrrhus. A deserter offered to the senate to poison King Pyrrhus. The senate and Gaius Fabricius handed the deserter over to Pyrrhus, their enemy.[17]

The story of Fabricius is told again more fully in Book III for a contrast with the base self-seeking acts of Marius and Gratidianus. Marius got the consulship by falsely accusing his own superior officer, Quintus Metellus, of criminal delay in the war against Jugurtha. He was made consul, but at the expense of good faith and justice. Gratidianus won the popular favor by publishing a vote of the praetors on the standardization of coinage before the time when the praetors had agreed on a public announcement of their policy. By his coup he secured treacherously all the glory of the act for himself but he failed in the duty of a good man.[18] These short, crisp accounts of notable actions of famous Romans unite in setting standards of conduct for young Marcus Cicero.

A few philosophical stories point abstract ideas. The theory of *decorum* or what is becoming, a concept so important to the Romans, is set off in a Greek story, pointed by a brief dialogue. When Pericles and Sophocles, the poet, were holding a joint command and had met on official business, Sophocles on seeing a beautiful boy passing, exclaimed : "What a handsome lad, Pericles !" Per-

---

[16] Cic. *de Off.* III. 99–110. [18] Cic. *de Off.* III. 79–81.
[17] Cic. *de Off.* I. 39–40 ; told also in III. 86–87.

icles replied : "Hush, Sophocles ! For it becomes a general to control not only his hands, but even his eyes." [19]

The conception of ideal friendship held by the philosophers is set forth in the story of two Pythagoreans, Damon and Phintias. When the tyrant, Dionysius, had condemned one of them to death and he had asked for a few days' respite in which to make arrangements for his dear ones, the other gave himself up as a hostage for his friend's return with the understanding that if he failed to appear, he himself would die in his place. When the condemned man returned on the day set, the tyrant admiring their good faith, begged to be enrolled as a third in their pact of friendship.[20] These two stories are typical of the rather simple discussions of abstract ethical concepts which appear in the *de Officiis*.

Stories from business life are more numerous. They are concerned with farm life, commercial transactions, problems of inheritance. An anecdote of old Cato has the flavor of Benjamin Franklin's aphorisms.[21]

When he was asked what was the most profitable feature of an estate, he replied : "Raising cattle successfully." What next to that ? "Raising cattle with fair success." And next ? "Raising cattle with but slight success." And fourth ? "Raising crops." And when his questioner said, "How about money-lending ?" Cato replied : "How about murder ?"

Criminal fraud, defined as "pretending one thing and practising another" [22] is illustrated by several anecdotes. Of these the most picturesque is on how Pythius of Syracuse sold a villa to Gaius Canius. When Canius, a Roman knight famous for his wit and culture, was taking a vacation at Syracuse, he let it be known that he wished

---

[19] Cic. *de Off*. I. 144.
[20] Cic. *de Off*. III. 45. See also Cic. *Tusc. Dis*. V. 63.

[21] Cic. *de Off*. II. 89, translated by Walter Miller in *The Loeb Classical Library*.
[22] Walter Miller's translation.

to buy a villa near there where he could entertain friends and enjoy himself without troublesome callers. A banker, Pythius, said he had a little country place that was not for sale to be sure, but Canius might use it if he wished and he invited him there to dinner the next day. After he accepted, Pythius, to whom men of all ranks were indebted as he was a money-lender, summoned some fishermen and requested them the next day to fish in front of his villa and he gave them full directions. Canius came to dinner on time. Pythius served a handsome feast. There was a fleet of boats before their eyes. Each fisherman brought in his catch and put down the fish before the feet of Pythius.

Then Canius said : "Tell me, Pythius, what is the meaning of all these fish and the fishing-boats ?" Pythius replied : "Nothing strange. In this place are all the fish in Syracuse. Here is fresh water. The fellows can't get along without this villa."

Canius was fired with desire for it and begged Pythius to sell it. He refused at first. There is no need of a long story. Canius got it. He was rich and he was so excited that he paid Pythius his price and bought the furniture too. The transaction was completed on the spot. The next day Canius invited his friends to it. He himself arrived early. He saw not even a thole-pin of a boat. He asked his nearest neighbor whether the fishermen had a holiday as he saw none of them.

"Not as far as I know," the other replied. "But the fellows don't usually fish here. So I was amazed at what went on yesterday." Canius was enraged, but what could he do ?

This is a lively story, told rapidly. It is varied by conversation. It is colored by subtle irony in the contrast between the cultured, leisure-loving Roman knight and the wily Greek money-lender. The moral point is however written in large letters at the end for Cicero's son :

So Pythius and all who do one thing and pretend another are treacherous, faithless, unprincipled men.[23]

This is a typical story on knavery in business dealings. The constant use of anecdotes in the *de Officiis* is explained by the fact that Cicero wrote it to his twenty-one year old son. Marcus wanted to be a soldier. At fourteen he had accompanied his father to Cilicia. At sixteen he had joined Pompey's army and commanded a division of cavalry with ability and distinction. In 45 B.C., he wished to fight in Spain under Caesar, but his father sent him to Greece to study and hoped to make him a philosopher instead of a soldier. So in this treatise on Moral Duties Cicero is giving instruction to Marcus in as pleasurable a way as possible. There is considerable evidence that Marcus' career as a student in Athens had made his father believe that such moral instruction was necessary.[24]

There has been the widest difference of opinion about the worth of the *de Officiis*. The Elder Pliny, Melanchthon, Erasmus, Frederick the Great lauded it to the skies. Mommsen damned it as a complete failure. Certainly it must be evaluated not as a philosophical treatise, but as a father's informal letters to a son in his student years. Then its simple, clear, ethical teachings and its picturesque, anecdotal style seem pure gold.

I purposely have avoided a chronological order in studying the use of anecdotes in Cicero's writings because the art-form he used rather than any period in his life seemed

23 Cic. *de Off.* III. 58–61. Compare the story of a sale of a house on the Caelian Hill III. 65–66 and the story of a forged will III. 72–74.

24 H. A. Holden, *de Officiis*, Introd. pp. xv–xvii.

to condition his narrative art. So we have gone from dialogue to philosophical lecture, to paternal letter. Now last of all I wish to take up the orations. In these, individual anecdotes are used judiciously and sparingly to point a moral or adorn a tale. Alexander at the tomb of Achilles exclaiming "O fortunate youth who found a Homer to proclaim your valor!" epitomizes the power poetry has to confer immortality.[25] The proper conduct of Roman envoys is set out as a lesson to the fear-stricken legates sent to Antony in the story of Popilius, legate to King Antiochus, who when the King delayed his reply to the Roman demands drew a circle around himself and told Antiochus that if he did not give his answer to Rome before he stepped out of the circle, he would report him to the senate.[26] These anecdotes may suffice to illustrate an *ornamentum,* and a *lumen.* But a study of such *exempla* in the orations would add nothing to the observations already made on the sources of Cicero's anecdotes, their style and functions.

His orations however in their use of *narratio* give us longer stories which demonstrate better than the miniature *exempla* the qualities of Cicero's narrative art. Of all the orations the Verrines are richest in the use of narratives. This is due to the very nature of the prosecution of Verres and to the fact that Cicero summoned all his powers of eloquence to combat the lawyer for the defense, Hortensius, the greatest orator of the day, and to establish his own career. Cicero's oratorical ability was on trial as much as Verres' character.

The prosecution of Verres took place in Rome in 70 B.C., at the end of his three years' service as Governor of Sicily. Cicero acted for the people of Sicily. The charge was technically one for restitution "of moneys claimed

[25] Cic. *pro Archia,* X. 24.   [26] Cic. *Phil.* VIII. 23.

back" and as such was tried before the Extortion Court which according to Sulla's Constitution was entirely composed of senators. During a provincial governor's term of office he had absolute power and could not be removed. Trials after return to Rome were usually quashed by a court of his peers. Reform of such senatorial monopoly of the courts had already been proposed in a bill providing that both knights and senators should constitute the Extortion Courts. The prosecution of Verres had therefore a larger political significance than the sentence of one governor to the payment of damages and the loss of his rights as a Roman citizen. It was part of the whole struggle between the orders for whose harmony Cicero worked so zealously.

To facilitate action, Cicero did not make the usual long opening speech, but used several short ones to introduce the material presented by witnesses and documents. The defense therefore had to follow the same procedure. So convincing was Cicero's array of charges in the *Actio Prima* that Verres fled into exile, and his condemnation and assessment for damages followed at once. Cicero however, to complete his presentation of the case, wrote the *Actio Secunda,* which was never delivered, as if it had been delivered and published it. Because it is then pure fiction it is an unusually significant source for a study of Cicero's art of narration. Cicero who was a *novus homo* in politics and a candidate for the aedileship at this time, with eager aspirations for the whole *cursus honorum,* after the trial of Verres was recognized as the greatest orator in Rome and his political career was assured. He had established his position by his stories of Verres' outrages against the Sicilians, stories so moving that they can still bring tears to the eyes of lovers of that fairest of islands.

In the Second Speech against Verres Cicero marshaled his charges under four heads : the quaestorship of Verres, his *legatio* in Asia, his praetorship in Rome, his propraetorship in Sicily. Cicero maintained that Verres' whole career was corrupt and he presents proof. Of course the great bulk of his charges is amassed from his governorship of Sicily. Stories of his previous brutality and robberies are concerned with such facts as his torture of a magistrate of Sicyon,[27] his robbery of Delos,[28] his seizure of a ship of the Roman navy from the quota furnished by Miletus.[29] The story of the girl of Lampsacum may be studied as typical of his early career.[30]

When Verres was in Asia as legate under the Governor of the province, Dolabella, he came on his travels to the town of Lampsacum on the Hellespont to the great calamity of the city. He was entertained by a certain Janitor and his companions were put up by other hosts. He had his usual spy, Rubrius, look around to see if there were any girl or woman on whose account he should delay his departure from the town. Rubrius reported that a certain leading citizen of Lampsacum named Philodamus, of fine family, great wealth, and distinguished position, had a beautiful unmarried daughter very modest and chaste who lived with her father. That report set Verres on fire. First he planned to move himself to Philodamus' house, but when his host, Janitor, took this as a slight and dissuaded him, he insisted on Philodamus' entertaining his tool, Rubrius, and in spite of Philodamus' protests installed Rubrius there by force. Philodamus as a gentleman then tried to show his usual hospitality and planned an elaborate dinner-party to which he urged Rubrius to invite whomever he wished, reserving only one place for

---

[27] Cic. *In C. Verrem.* II. 1, 45.
[28] Cic. *In C. Verr.* II. 1, 46–48.
[29] Cic. *In C. Verr.* II. 1, 86–87.
[30] Cic. *In C. Verr.* II. 1, 63–85.

himself.   Philodamus sent his young son off to dinner
with a kinsman.   Rubrius invited all Verres' staff and
Verres informed them what they were to do.

As the dinner progressed the host urged them to drink
with him in the Greek fashion and over the goblets there
was much gaiety. Suddenly Rubrius cried out : "A question, Philodamus.   Why do you not order your daughter
to be called here to us ?"   The dignified, elderly host was
struck dumb with horror at the rascal's suggestion, but
Rubrius kept insisting.   Philodamus then said that it was
not the custom of the Greeks to have their women re-
cline at banquets with men.   Then someone else shouted
out : "Really, this is intolerable !   Have the girl brought
in !" At the same moment Rubrius ordered that the front
door should be closed and guarded by his slaves.

Philodamus then perceiving that the rape of his daughter was planned, summoned his own slaves and told them
to pay no attention to himself, but to defend his daughter
and he ordered that one should go to tell his son what
was happening.

There was a free fight in the whole house.   And between the slaves of Rubrius and of his host, Philodamus,
a gentleman of the highest rank and character, was
mauled about in his own home.   Rubrius even threw
boiling water over him.   At the news of the riot his son
hastened home, almost beside himself, to try to save his
father's life and his sister's honor.   Moreover all the people of Lampsacum on learning the outrage gathered at
the house.   In the mêlée Verres' lictor, Cornelius, who
had been deputed by Verres to carry off the girl with the
aid of the slaves, was killed.   Some slaves were wounded.
Rubrius was injured.   Verres since he saw what a tumult
his lust had aroused only wanted to get away.

The inhabitants of Lampsacum were so indignant that

they assembled at the house where Verres was staying and started to burn it down. They were stopped only by the persuasion of a number of Roman citizens in Lampsacum on business who urged that they should respect Verres' official position, although the man was a corrupt scoundrel ; they urged that since he had not accomplished what he had attempted and would not be at Lampsacum in the future, their culpability would be less if they spared a scoundrel than if they killed a legate. So Verres escaped destruction.

Verres however never dared to state the true reason for the riot or invent a false one. All the same Philodamus and his son were put on trial and sentenced to death. What sort of sentence was that ? Hear the story, gentlemen, and pity our allies. Since the slaying of the man who was Verres' lictor in name, but who was in truth the instrument of his criminal passion, Verres feared that Philodamus would be acquitted and eventually go to Rome and ruin him. He therefore persuaded the governor, Dolabella, to leave his army and province and come to the trial. Dolabella did and he and all his staff were made members of the court by Nero as indeed was Verres himself. The people were then so terrorized that Philodamus could not get anyone to defend him. Nevertheless in the first trial the opinion of the court was that the case was not proved. At the second hearing under the pressure of Dolabella and Verres, Philodamus and his son were condemned to death. Dolabella urged immediate execution.

Then in the forum of Laodicea there was a cruel and heartrending scene. An aged father was executed because he had defended the chastity of his children, a son because he had defended his father's life and his sister's honor. Each wept for the death of the other. What

tears do you suppose Nero shed? What weeping was
there through all Asia? What grief and muttering at
Lampsacum at the thought that two innocent men had
been beheaded, men of high rank, allies and friends of
the Roman people, on account of a scoundrel's unspeak-
able wickedness and uncontrolled lust?

This is the real end of the telling of the story but
Cicero went on to establish the facts by documentary evidence of letters and of records of the trial until he proved
that Verres had originally accused two other men of
starting the fire and had never dared bring the alleged
insults to a Roman legate to Rome. The evidence in
this case alone should have damned Verres' character.

Actually that must have been Cicero's reason for telling this story at such length in his accusations. The case
has really nothing else to do with the prosecution of Verres for extortion from the Sicilians. But it is a master-
piece of the use of character-drawing and pathos to arouse
the indignation of the court and of the hearers.

The simple, rapid narrative begins with a description
of the quiet town of Lampsacum on the Hellespont with
its peace-loving, self-respecting citizens. The story of
Verres' fatal visit to it is worked up gradually to the climax of horror at the dinner-party when two remarks (the
only conversation used) reveal to the unsuspecting host
the perfidy and lust of his Roman guest. The most subtle
irony is used in the narrative. Cicero's audience, like the
spectators in a Greek tragedy, knew from Verres' character what the catastrophe was to be, but Philodamus had
no idea of it. A still finer irony is used in giving the
insulted Greek all the standards of hospitality and family
purity that belonged to the old Roman traditions and
showing that every one of them was outraged by a Roman
legate. The pathos in the story centers in a girl who

never appears.   The thought of her is always present and part of the horror of the story is that her ultimate fate after the execution of her father and brother is not told. On the foundation of this violation of the sanctity of family life Cicero builds up his strongest appeal to the court : an immoral scoundrel like Verres impairs by his conduct as legate the whole reputation of Rome for justice to her allies.

From such stories of wrongs inflicted on Eastern provinces, Cicero moves the scene to Rome and shows how Verres' avarice made him ruin a young ward for the sake of money, a scandal connected with the contract for the upkeep of the Temple of Castor when Verres transferred the contract to a higher bidder on the ground that the columns had not been kept exactly perpendicular.[31]   Cicero here varied his method by telling how at the trial the defrauded boy stood beside his uncle as he gave his evidence so that the sight of the impoverished lad brought tears to the eyes of all fathers of young children who were in the court-room.

The most moving stories in the Verrines however are those about Verres' thefts and crimes in Sicily.   In Book IV there are stories of robberies of works of art from individuals (Roman citizens and foreign princes), and from famous cities in Sicily (Segesta, Tyndaris, Henna).   Book V turns to records of barbarous treatment of Roman citizens in the island.   The first chapter of Book IV, *de Signis*, presents the sweeping charge of Verres' robberies.

In all Sicily, so rich, so ancient a province, in its many wealthy towns, and families, there was no silver vase, no piece of Corinthian or Delian bronze, no jewel or pearl, no *objet d'art* made of gold or ivory, no statue of bronze, marble or ivory, no painting, no textile, which Verres did not track down, inspect and steal if it pleased him.[32]   In such a state of affairs men could save their

[31] Cic. *In C. Verr.* II. 1, 130–54.   [32] Cic. *In C. Verr.* II. 4, 1.

family heirlooms only by ingenuity : Pamphilus paid a large sum
to Verres' experts to have them declare his scyphoi worthless pieces
of pottery instead of silver.[33]   Diodorus had his silver shipped secretly from city to city and himself went into exile at Rome for
the three years of Verres' governorship.[34]   But the young Syrian
prince, son of King Antiochus, was too ingenuous to suspect the
Roman governor before he was fleeced.   He was robbed of silver
plate, golden goblets, a wine-ladle carved out of a single gem,
worst of all of a be-jewelled candelabrum which Syria had sent as a
dedication to Jupiter Capitolinus in Rome.[35]   No religious scruple
stayed Verres' hands from robbing the gods.   He even carried off
from a shrine in the house of Gaius Heius of Messana a marble Cupid of Praxiteles and a bronze statue of Hercules, both art treasures
of the city and objects of worship in a private chapel as the altars
placed in front of them proved.   With irony Cicero concludes :
"The famous Cupid did not seek the home of the notorious pro-
curer and the rule of his mistresses ; he was content with that family shrine.   He knew he had been willed to Heius by his fore-
fathers as part of his sacred inheritance ; he did not seek Verres,
the heir of a courtesan." [36]

The religious indignation evoked by the stories of Heius
and the Syrian prince is intensified by the tales of the
thefts from cities, of the statue of Diana from Segesta, of
Mercury from Tyndaris, of Ceres from Henna.   In these
stories of sacrilege Cicero uses a masterly power of vivid
description to present to our eyes the cities of the island,
each with its own traditions and beauties, and the statues
which they treasured.   His pictorial technique impresses
vivid images on our minds : the scene when the statue of
Diana the young huntress bearing quiver and torch was
carried out of Segesta while all the matrons and girls es-
corted her to their frontier, sprinkling her with perfumes,
covering her with garlands and flowers, burning incense
about her ;[37] or the torture of Sopater, the mayor of Tyndaris, stripped naked, mounted astride the bronze equestrian statue of Gaius Marcellus in the forum, tied and left

[33] Cic. *In C. Verr*. II. 4, 32–33.   [36] Cic. *In C. Verr*. II. 4, 3–8.
[34] Cic. *In C. Verr*. II. 4, 38–41.   [37] Cic. *In C. Verr*. II. 4, 72–79.
[35] Cic. *In C. Verr*. II. 4, 60–71.

there in midwinter in pouring cold rain until the senate
of Tyndaris promised Verres their statue of Mercury ; [38]
or the violated sanctity of Henna, that high acropolis
dominating a plain of lakes and groves and perennial flowers, Henna where Dis carried off the Maid, Henna which
Ceres her mother visited in her search for the girl bring-
ing it the gift of corn, Henna where Ceres lives forever
and is so cherished that all the inhabitants seem not citizens but priests, acolytes, servants of the goddess.[39]   Here
descriptive art creates reality that is visible, is tangible.
And the beauty of the descriptions intensifies the horror
of the sacrileges committed.

In Book V, *de Suppliciis,* story after story could be cited
as striking illustrations of Cicero's narrative art, for example the false accusation and imprisonment of Apollonius of Panhormus and his release on payment of large
sums, a case deliberately planned for the terrorization of
all wealthy citizens of Sicily ; [40] and Verres' unjust execution of the captains of the Roman fleet in the war with the
pirates, narratives rich in dramatic scenes of horror.[41] But
perhaps the last story in the Verrines may serve to demonstrate Cicero's use of narration in depicting Verres' brutalities to Roman citizens.[42]

The story of Gavius of Consa is such, Cicero says, that
the facts speak for themselves and need no eloquence to
inflame the hearts of hearers.   Gavius was one of the Roman citizens whom Verres threw into prison in the Stone
Quarries.   Somehow he escaped and came to Messana.
There he made the mistake of talking openly about his
wrongs and declaring that he was going straight to Rome
and would be ready for Verres when he arrived there.
Spies heard him (Messana was the one town in Sicily that

[38] Cic. *In C. Verr.* II. 4, 84–87.
[39] Cic. *In C. Verr.* II. 4, 107–111.
[40] Cic. *In C. Verr.* II. 5, 16–24.
[41] Cic. *In C. Verr.* II. 5, 83–132.
[42] Cic. *In C. Verr.* II. 5, 158–70.

supported Verres in every way).   Gavius was arrested and what he had said was reported to Verres on his arrival that same day.

There was no trial.   Verres mad with rage declared that Gavius was a spy from the fugitive army and had him stripped, tied and flogged in the forum though Gavius kept crying out, "I am a Roman citizen," and shrieked that he had served in the Roman army under Lucius Raecius who was then at Panhormus and would identify him. Verres did not wait to investigate.   After further torture of his victim with fire and hot metal plates he had him crucified and, as a refinement of barbarous cruelty, he had the cross set up looking across the straits and declared that he selected that spot so that a fellow who claimed to be a Roman citizen might from the cross look to Italy and his home.

Cicero's indignation here becomes eloquence in spite of himself :

It is a crime to bind a Roman citizen, an outrage to flog him, to put him to death almost murder.   What then is it to crucify him ?   Such a horror cannot be described by any word.   That fiend was not content with all these cruelties.   "Let him look at his country," he cried.   "Let him die with a vision of his laws and liberty before his eyes."   On that spot it was not Gavius, one humble man, whom you crucified, Verres, but the whole cause of freedom for Roman citizens.

In this story Cicero by a bare recital of facts leads up to a climax of indignation addressed in the name of liberty to all Roman citizens.   His concise, simple telling of a story shaped to appeal to those who believed in the fundamental rights of life and liberty is eloquence itself.

Cicero's case was now completed.   He had only to beg the judges to vote as their intelligence and their honor dictated.   Then he turned in his peroration to all the gods and goddesses on whose temples and worships an impious madman had waged unholy war and asked them to hear and bless his prayer for a just verdict.

I have tried in this long chapter to give a clear picture of Cicero's art of narration by many illustrations of it. For this purpose I selected out of the vast amount of material in his writings the works which are most significant for the subject in themselves and by comparison with each other. So the Dialogue on Old Age gave samples of small, illustrative anecdotes centered on sayings or acts of famous men, stories largely from Greek sources, brief, concise, pointed, told in everyday language to enrich the conversation. In the *Tusculan Disputations,* Socratic dialogues between a master and his pupils, wherein Cicero really lectured in the form of a *declamatio,* many *exempla* were assembled to teach young men how to live happily. These too were taken from the Greek, were told by sayings or deeds, but always with a philosophical point and there is such a wealth of them that they are often used in series, one anecdote piled upon another either with the same point or a slight variant.

The *de Officiis,* a letter on Moral Duties addressed to Cicero's twenty-one year old son, is the richest storehouse of anecdotes in all Cicero's writings. In its skillful use of stories drawn from mythology, from Greek and Roman history, from philosophy, from business life it demonstrates how Cicero could make instruction pleasurable and memorable by concrete pictures of ideas conveyed.

Then Cicero's art was studied in those longer stories in his Orations which were called *narrationes* and the particular oration selected for consideration was the *Actio Secunda* of the Verrines because, since that was never delivered, yet was written as though it were delivered, it belongs to the realm of pure fiction [43] and with no limitation of set time that an actual court-room might demand gave Cicero opportunity to use his narrative art to the full. Here with unsparing realism, in plain language quickly moving to a climax, he presents stories of Verres' crimes of brutality, lust, and avarice. Pictorial descriptions, subtle character-drawing, artful irony, emotional appeal vary his narratives. The audience of his readers is aroused to their noblest sentiments of humanity, patriotism and religion. And through the force of Cicero's art of narration justice was done to the wronged Sicilians, a reform of provincial government was started, and Cicero was recognized as the first orator in Rome. Later on he was to make another reputation in his rhetorical and philosophical writings. Through all these forms he may easily be seen today in a more human aspect as the prince of story-tellers.

[43] Émile Thomas, *Cicéron Verrines,* Paris, 1894, p. 20.

III

HISTORY FROM EXEMPLA :
LIVY'S USE OF ANECDOTES

THE reading of the extant books of Livy's history, *ab Urbe Condita,* unveils a life-like portrait of the author. In many passages, the historian steps out of the pattern of his history into a personal address to his reader as the chorus in Greek tragedy through the Parabasis spoke directly to the audience in the theater.   This self-revelation affords us a knowledge of Livy's attitude towards his history, for he discusses his subject-matter and his sources, shows his awareness of the technique of his art and, by comments on the course of events, the characters of persons, and the worship of the gods, paints as vivid a self-portrait as did the brush of many a Renaissance Italian artist.

The most significant passage for the understanding of Livy is the preface to the first book.   Here he shudders at the magnitude of the task of tracing the history of Rome for over seven hundred years, yet thrills at the memory of the noble days of old in whose contemplation he may escape from the evils of his own time.   He reviews the stuff of which his history is to be made : myths, moral standards, the men and the policies in peace and war by which empire was acquired and extended, finally the decline of order and discipline.

In this review of subject matter he makes clear that to

him myths are poetic stories not supported by historical records ; therefore he will not affirm or refute them, he will rather tell them not for their importance but for their splendor.   The real value of writing history is in his eyes to give moral instruction.

What chiefly makes the study of history wholesome and profitable is this, that you behold the lessons of every kind of experience set forth as on a conspicuous monument ; from these you may choose for yourself and for your own state what to imitate, from these mark for avoidance what is shameful in the conception and shameful in the result.   For the rest, either love of the task I have set myself deceives me, or no state was ever greater, none more righteous or richer in good examples, none ever where avarice and luxury came into the social order so late, or where humble means and thrift were so highly esteemed and so long held in honour.[1]

These *bona exempla,* the storied treasure of old Rome, with their salubrious values, are to be Livy's offering to his own time in its moral illness, its decay, its impending ruin.   And with a sense of a devout physician's responsibility he offers at the end of his preface a prayer to the gods and goddesses that with good omens they would bless the great work to which he has put his hand.

In another preface, at the beginning of the account of the Punic Wars,[2] Livy again exalts the magnitude of his task, in recording a war that was the most memorable of all wars ever waged because of the strength of the two combating nations, their intense antagonism, their varying fortunes.   And at the end of his narrative of this great struggle,[3] he breathes a sigh of relief as if, he says, he had shared the labor and the danger.   And as a sort of apology for his fatigue, he confesses that he is being swept off his feet into unfathomed depths like men who,

[1] Livy, 1. *Preface,* translated by B. O. Foster, in *The Loeb Classical Library.*

[2] 21, 1.

[3] 31, 1.

after wading in shallows near the shore, advance too far and are carried away. And he had yet to record other wars at home and abroad : struggles between patricians and plebeians in the city, battles among little states in the peninsula and more foreign wars as the east came nearer to Rome and the eternal conflict between east and west caught Rome in its toils.

In the progress of his writing, the difficulties about his sources were as stupendous as the magnitude of his theme. The historian could content himself with neither affirming nor denying the reliability of the myths in the earliest history.   But for the time of the early Republic he covets written records, yet cannot find them, for even such brief ones as existed in the commentaries of the pontiffs and other public and private documents perished for the most part in the burning of the city.[4]

Then as he proceeds hopefully to clearer and more certain events, he finds that contemporary historians are lacking ; it is difficult to choose between conflicting authorities and moreover records like funeral orations and inscriptions under portraits are unreliable since families sought glory by mendacious claims of honors.[5]   When he can forsake the annalists and take up Polybius, he is on surer ground and has richer material.[6]   Since no question about Livy's history has aroused more controversy than this one of his use of sources, it is fair to state briefly that he recognized clearly his own difficulties.

His awareness of the technique of his art is as apparent

[4] For a refutation of this traditional belief see Lucy G. Roberts, "The Gallic Fire and Roman Archives" in *Memoirs of the American Academy in Rome,* vol. II. 1918, pp. 55–65.

[5] Livy, 8, 40. For Livy's use of sources, see A. Klotz, (9), T. Livius, in Pauly-Wissowa, *Real-Encyclopädie der classischen Altertumswissenschaft,* 13, Stuttgart, 1926, 816–852 ; also H. Peter, *Historicorum Romanorum Reliquiae,* volumen prius[2], Lipsiae 1914.

[6] See G. De Sanctis, *Storia dei Romani,* Vol. III. *L'età delle guerre Puniche.* Parte II. Torino, 1917, *inter alios.*

as his consciousness of the magnitude of his task and the perplexities of his sources.   New historians, he says, are always trying to surpass in the art of writing the crude, archaic style of the ancients.[7]   Livy comments too on the style of various orators : Tempanius made a speech that was unpolished, but had a military dignity.[8]   Menenius Agrippa persuaded the plebs to return to Rome after their secession by the story of the body and the belly which he told in the ancient, rough style.[9]   And a dashing incident of the siege of Veii is mentioned by Livy as more fit to be presented in the theater which delights in marvels than to be believed.[10]   These brief comments would be convincing evidence of Livy's sensitivity to style even if his own varied technique in writing his great history did not display the consummate artist.

The repeated discussions as to whether Livy was a greater artist than an historian seem futile in view of the pageant of Roman history which he has made pass before our eyes.   If the style is the man, as Walter Pater affirmed, then the artist merges with the old Roman whose spirit appears in his intense nationalism, his praise of traditional military and civic virtues, his recognition of the vitality of the struggle between patricians and plebeians in which individual liberty was at stake, his moral earnestness and his religious reverence.   The essential truth of Livy's history is an inner quality which with a fine literary conscience interprets the spirit of Rome to his own time and to future generations.

To understand how the artist-historian achieved this interpretation we must return to those *bona exempla* which he says in his preface are the fruitful and life-giving material of true history.   We must see what sort of *ex-*

[7] 1. *Preface.*
[8] 4, 41.
[9] 2, 32.
[10] 5, 21.

empla, or anecdotes, he selects and how he treats them.
Many are concerned with religion and have to do with
omens, prodigies, miracles, and the appeasement of the
gods.   Others depict the social life of various periods and
are therefore concerned with women and the important
part they played in the state.   Political life furnishes
stories of struggles between the social orders in Rome,
patricians and plebeians, and character sketches of powerful old aristocrats and new men of striking ability.   Then
as the history of Rome sweeps on from Republic to Empire, ever-increasing warfare for expansion in Italy, for
the conquest of Carthage, for extension of colonies east-
ward is narrated with an epic color of heroic battles.   For
the glamour and the horror of war were never presented
with more splendor and more realism than by Livy.   In
short stories ranging from myths to duels, from the taking of a little mound to the slaughter of the one hundred
and six Fabii, and in long narratives, told as inserts or
serials, Livy paints his war pictures.   These stories of
wars outweigh all his others, in short, are the background
for all his history.

Cicero had recognized the similarity of history to oratory in the use of narratives, descriptions, and speeches.[11]
Cicero too in a long letter to Lucceius [12] had developed a
theory of monographs as inserts in long histories and had
shown the use of such a story in varying the development
of chronological annals.   The adduced value of such inserts is not impaired by the fact that Cicero is persuading
Lucceius to proceed at once to his own story "from the

---

[11] Cicero, *Orator,* 19, 65. (Sophis-
tae) a re saepe discedunt, intexunt
fabulas. . . Huic generi historia fini-
tima est, in qua et narratur ornate et
regio saepe aut pugna describitur;
interponuntur etiam contiones et
hortationes.

[12] Cicero, *ad Fam.,* V. 12. The
translation of the Letters of Cicero
by Evelyn S. Shuckburgh is used, vol.
I. pp. 228-29.

beginning of the conspiracy to my return from exile."
"Truly," he says, "the mere chronological record of the
annals has very little charm for us — little more than the
entries in the *fasti* : but the doubtful and varied fortunes
of a man, frequently of eminent character, involve feelings of wonder, suspense, joy, sorrow, hope, fear : if these
fortunes are crowned with a glorious death, the imagination is satisfied with the most fascinating delight which
reading can give."

A perfect illustration of such an insert-monograph in
Livy's history is the story of Demetrius, son of Philip V
of Macedon.[13]   And these longer narratives as well as the
short anecdotes form so fundamental a part of Livy's style
that some critics have attributed his greatness to an epic
quality of narration, the piling up of picture after picture,
action after action, others to the dramatic quality of his
short and vivid episodes.[14]   Of course, no study of his
narrative art could be completed without a consideration
of his use of fictitious speeches for character drawing and
emotional effects.   But his use of the oration demands
and has received separate treatment [15] so here only those
speeches will be considered which form a significant part
of some anecdote or narration.

Livy ended his preface with an appeal to the gods to
prosper his work.   This study of his anecdotes is to begin
with stories of religious awe.   For, though war is almost
the continuous background of Livy's history, all through
it the horrors of war are intensified by the dread of angry
gods.   Over and over the consuls cannot leave the city for

[13] Livy, 39, 35, 47–48, 53 ; 40, 5–16,
20–24, 54–56. See C. F. Edson, "Perseus and Demetrius," in *Harvard
Studies in Classical Philology*, 46
(1935), 191–202.
[14] K. Witte, "Ueber die Form der
Darstellung in Livius Geschichts-
werk," in *Rhenisches Museum für
Philologie*, 65 (1910), 270–305, 359–
419.
[15] For example, see Ragnar Ull-
mann, *La technique des discours dans
Salluste, Tite Live et Tacite. La ma-
tière et la composition*. Oslo, 1927.

military action or battles must be postponed because of ill
omens and appalling prodigies.   The history of the people cannot be presented without a picture of the deep-
rooted fear of heaven that constantly beset them.

To the devout and the superstitious, natural phenomena were signs of the gods' displeasure.   Thunder-
storms were ominous and there were constant reports of
bolts that struck city walls and gates,[16] shops,[17] ships in
harbor,[18] men and beasts.[19]   Perhaps even more terrifying was the fact that a symbol of victory, the *columna
rostrata Aemiliana,* was smitten.[20]   And worst of all were
the reports of lightning that smote the temples and statues
of the gods.[21]   Phenomenal fires in the sky too were seen :
a blaze like a torch sweeping from east to west,[22] two suns
at night,[23] an altar in the sky.[24]

Manifestations on earth included earthquakes, one
even repeated for thirty-eight days,[25] droughts,[26] floods
of the Tiber river [27] and the Alban Lake,[28] showers of
stones,[29] of earth,[30] of flesh,[31] of blood,[32] epidemics, which
constantly recurred,[33] and accidents.   The last include
the fall of huge stones from the Capitol into the Vicus
Iugarius, which killed several people,[34] and the collapse
of a mast in the Circus.[35]

Equally horrifying prodigies were monstrosities that
were born : a lamb with two heads,[36] a lamb with two

[16] 24, 44 ; 27, 11 ; 29, 14 ; 30, 38 ;
35, 21 ; 41, 16.
[17] 30, 38.
[18] 36, 37.
[19] 22, 36 ; 33, 26.
[20] 42, 20.
[21] 24, 7, 11 and 28 ; 36, 37 ; 37, 3 ;
39, 22 ; 40, 2 ; 41, 16.
[22] 21, 14.
[23] 21, 14.
[24] 24, 10.
[25] 34, 55 ; 35, 40 ; 40, 59.
[26] 4, 30.

[27] 30, 38 ; 35, 9 and 21.
[28] 5, 15–19.
[29] 22, 36 ; 29, 10 ; 30, 38 ; 35, 9 ;
39, 22.
[30] 37, 3 ; 45, 16.
[31] 3, 10.
[32] 34, 45 ; 39, 46 and 56 ; 40, 19.
[33] 3, 6 ; 4, 25 ; 5, 13 ; 7, 2 ; 40,
19.
[34] 35, 21.
[35] 39, 7.
[36] 32, 9.

heads and five feet,[37] a lamb with an udder full of milk,[38] a mule with three feet,[39] a foal with five feet,[40] a pig with a human head,[41] three chickens with three feet each,[42] a snake with four legs.[43] More dreadful were human monstrosities : a child born without hands and feet,[44] a child without eyes and nose,[45] a child with the face of an elephant.[46] Worst of all were the hermaphrodites,[47] which must be executed at once.

To minds that interpreted such natural phenomena, such monstrosities as signs of the displeasure of the gods, unusual circumstances were interpreted as miracles. With awe it was reported that a wolf ran through Rome,[48] a vulture appeared in a temple at Caere,[49] a swarm of bees settled in the forum of Casinum,[50] and of Capua,[51] birds forsook their nests in a religious precinct,[52] sea-serpents were seen gamboling in the ocean,[53] two cows walked upstairs.[54] And credence grew until the impossible was reported as actual. A brazen heifer was impregnated by a wild bull.[55] Statues sweated blood,[56] or wept,[57] or grew hair.[58] Four standards sweated blood.[59] A laurel tree sprang up on the poop of a war-ship.[60]

Ears no less than eyes were betrayed by terror so that various miraculous voices were reported. A cow spoke.[61] An ox cried : *Roma, cave tibi.*[62] An unborn child shouted : *Io, Triumphe !* [63]

[37] 32, 29.
[38] 27, 4.
[39] 40, 2 and 45.
[40] 32, 1.
[41] 27, 4; 32, 9.
[42] 32, 1.
[43] 41, 9.
[44] 34, 45.
[45] 41, 9.
[46] 27, 11.
[47] 27, 11 ; 31, 12 ; 39, 22.
[48] 32, 29 ; 41, 9.
[49] 27, 23.
[50] 27, 23.

[51] 35, 9.
[52] 27, 4.
[53] 27, 4.
[54] 36, 37.
[55] 41, 13.
[56] 22, 36 ; 23, 31.
[57] 40, 19.
[58] 32, 1.
[59] 27, 4.
[60] 32, 1.
[61] 3, 10 ; 41, 13.
[62] 35, 21.
[63] 24, 10.

When the Romans had waged an indecisive battle against the people of Veii and Tarquinii, in the silence of the next night a mighty voice was heard in the Arsian forest, believed to be the voice of Silvanus, which proclaimed that one more of the Tuscans had fallen in the battle and the Romans had conquered.[64]   One night a Roman plebeian heard a voice on the Nova Via which foretold that the Gauls were coming.[65]   When the Latins were burning the town of Satricum, a voice from the temple of Mater Matuta ordered them with dire threats to keep the fires from her shrine.[66]

Voices too might be accompanied by apparitions : in a dream, the dead might speak, or a mystic figure utter a prophecy.   Romulus, descending from heaven at dawn, appeared to Proculus Julius and gave him this message : "Go announce to the Romans that the gods will that my Rome should be the head of the world ; therefore they should cherish military science and know and teach their descendants that no human power can withstand Roman arms." [67]   When Hannibal was on the march in Spain, he had a dreadful vision.   In a dream a divine youth appeared to him and declared that he had been sent to lead Hannibal into Italy so the general must follow him and never look backward.   Hannibal in terror followed, but at last his anxiety about what was behind him forced him to turn his eyes and he saw a huge serpent following amid falling trees and crashing thunder.   This horror he was told was the Devastation of Italy, but he must go forward and let fate take its secret course.[68]

Now all such visions, voices, miracles, prodigies, omens might be reported incorrectly or even created by the fear that is so terrible a part of war psychology.   But when

[64] 2, 7.
[65] 5, 32 and 50.
[66] 6, 33.

[67] 1, 16.
[68] 21, 22.

religious ceremonies which were officially conducted and sacrosanct were interrupted by bad omens, the national depression was black indeed. The sacred chickens refused to eat.[69] Livers of victims sacrificed wasted away before inspection or snakes devoured them.[70] Part of a religious formula was inadvertently omitted.[71] At a *lectisternium* the gods on the couches turned away their heads and a platter set before Jupiter fell on the floor.[72] Worst of all, perhaps, the holy fire in the temple of Vesta went out.[73]

All these evil omens were signs of the gods' displeasure and demanded that in some way offended deities must be appeased. Certain forms of satisfaction were obvious. Monstrosities must be exterminated, even hermaphrodites.[74] A vestal who let the fire go out was flogged to death.[75] Sacrifices must be offered of full-grown victims or of the little unweaned ones. Numbers of victims must be multiplied according to the sin, so that once fifty goats were sacrificed,[76] and in case of particular horror a *ver sacrum* would be proclaimed, and all the young animals born in a certain period be offered up.[77] Once, indeed, even human sacrifice was deemed necessary.[78] Then prayers, *supplicationes,* at some shrine or at all the temples were ordered for a certain number of days. A banquet might be spread for the gods, and often was after the first *lectisternium* in 399 B.C.[79] Temples were vowed.[80] Games were instituted.[81] New gods were brought to Rome at the order of the Sibylline Books to save the state.[82] To such desperate and expensive precautions

[69] 27, 16.
[70] 41, 15 ; 25, 16–17.
[71] 41, 16.
[72] 40, 59.
[73] 28, 11.
[74] 39, 22.
[75] 28, 11.

[76] 45, 16.
[77] 22, 9–10 ; 34, 44.
[78] 22, 57.
[79] 5, 13 ; 7, 2.
[80] 4, 25 ; 35, 9.
[81] 7, 2 ; 25, 12.
[82] 10, 47 ; 29, 10, 11 and 14.

did men's terrors drive them in time of epidemic, famine, and war.

Against such a background of fear and appeasement Livy tells story after story concerned with religion.   A flame appears on the head of a sleeping slave boy in a palace.[83]   Queen Tanaquil, skilled in augury as all Etruscan women are, lets it burn out and from its brilliant light prophesies the future greatness of this captive lad who is to be King Servius Tullius.   A snake glides out of a wooden column in the palace of King Tarquinius of Rome and the king aghast sends his sons and nephew, Brutus, to the oracle at Delphi to ascertain the meaning of this awful omen.   On that embassy, Brutus, the clever dullard, learned that he was to hold the highest power in Rome for since the oracle conferred that boon on the one who should first kiss his mother, Brutus pretended to fall down and touched his lips to earth recognizing her as the common mother of all mortals.[84]

A dream might be as significant as portents.   Once when the great games were being prepared in Rome, early in the morning before they began, a certain citizen drove a slave under a yoke across the Circus, flogging him as he went.   Then the games began.   Not long after a plebeian, Titus Latinius, had a dream in which Jupiter appeared to him and said he had been offended by the dancer at the games and unless they were repeated, a calamity would befall the city ; he was to announce this to the consuls.   When Latinius in awe of the magistrates, did not report his dream, in a few days he lost his son.   A second time the same vision appeared.   When he still delayed to report it, he fell very ill himself.   Then at last on the advice of his kinsmen, he was carried on a litter to the consuls and into the senate to give the message of the god, and

[83] 1. 39.   [84] 1. 56.

when he had performed his duty a great miracle happened for he regained the use of his limbs and was able to walk home. The games which had been begun with the ill omen of the scourged slave (Jupiter's "dancer") were repeated with great magnificence.[85]

These early stories and others like them are told simply and reverently as facts.   But even in the time of the kings Livy's rationalization of myths appears in his two versions of the disappearance of Romulus from earth.[86]   And as the history of Rome progresses, Livy comments more and more on the susceptibility and gullibility of mankind, reveals how humor creeps into their dealings with the gods and finally late in his history, explains the personal awe with which he has related these awful stories.

When Lucius Annius Setinus, after pleading in vain to the Romans for the rights of the Latins whom he represented, had defied Rome's greatest god, Jupiter, he slipped as he left the temple, fell down the steps, and fainted, or as some say, was killed.   Livy says that all authorities do not agree about his death or about the crash of thunder that accompanied his fall, "for these things can be true or neat inventions to portray vividly the wrath of the gods." [87]

A melodramatic religious story is the *devotio* or religious self-sacrifice of Decius Mus.[88]   In the battle of Vesuvius between the Latins and the Romans, the Roman side was retreating.   The consul Decius decided to appease the gods by offering up himself.   This was an old custom and for a *devotio* there was a particular ritual.

In the confusion of this movement Decius the consul called out to Marcus Valerius in a loud voice : "We have need of Heaven's

[85] 2, 36–37.
[86] 1, 16.
[87] 8, 6.

[88] 8, 9–11. The quoted translations from chapters 9 and 11 are by B. O. Foster, in *The Loeb Classical Library.*

help, Marcus Valerius. Come therefore, state pontiff of the
Roman people, dictate the words, that I may devote myself to
save the legions." The pontiff bade him don the purple-bordered
toga, and with veiled head and one hand thrust out from the toga
and touching his chin, stand upon a spear that was laid under
his feet, and say as follows : "Janus, Jupiter, Father Mars, Quiri-
nus, Bellona, Lares, divine Novensiles, divine Indigites, ye gods
in whose power are both we and our enemies, and you, divine
Manes — I invoke and worship you, I beseech and crave your
favour, that you prosper the might and the victory of the Roman
People of the Quirites, and visit the foes of the Roman People of
the Quirites with fear, shuddering, and death. As I have pro-
nounced the words, even so in behalf of the republic of the Roman
People of the Quirites, and of the army, the legions, the auxiliaries
of the Roman People of the Quirites, do I devote the legions and
auxiliaries of the enemy, together with myself, to the divine Manes
and to Earth."

After this prayer the consul leaped on his horse and
plunged into the midst of the enemy. He seemed more
august than human as if sent from heaven to appease all
the wrath of the gods. Everywhere he went, he caused
terror and panic and when he died, pierced by many weapons, the Latins were routed.

Livy gives many more details of the ritual for such self-
sacrifice of a general or of an appointed substitute for
himself. At the end he says :

These particulars, even though the memory of every religious
and secular usage has been wiped out by men's preference of the
new and outlandish to the ancient and homebred, I have thought
it not foreign to my purpose to repeat, and in the very words in
which they were formulated and handed down.

The story is told with careful accuracy of quotation of
ritual and prayer, with dramatic description of the psy-
chological effects of the human sacrifice, and with the
author's own comment on his wish to preserve the record
of such sacred, ancient custom.

In contrast to such devout and serious narratives are

certain religious anecdotes in which a lively humor is displayed.   A touch of this appears in the early story of the capture of Veii.[89]   When chosen youths were moving the statue of Juno from her temple, one of them, either inspired by the gods or in youthful jest, asked "Do you wish to go to Rome, Juno ?" and the others all shouted that the goddess had nodded !   A more grim humor appears in the account of how the consul, Lucius Papirius, treated unfavorable omens.[90]   In the war with the Samnites, the whole Roman army was so eager for battle, that even a keeper of the sacred chickens was so affected that when the birds refused to eat, he dared falsify the auspices and announce to the consul that the corn had danced before them as they pecked at it.   The joyful consul had ordered battle when the rumor that the omens had been falsified came to the ears of the consul's nephew, Spurius.   As he was a youth (Livy comments) who was born before the learning that rejects the gods, he reported the rumor to his uncle. The consul after thanking him said that, as he had been told the corn had danced, the auspices were favorable for the Roman people and the army.   But he then ordered the centurions to place the keepers of the chickens in the front ranks.   Before the battle actually began, the guilty keeper of the chickens was hit by a flying javelin and fell dead.   The consul exclaimed : "The gods are in the battle : the guilty has paid the penalty !"   A raven croaked assent.   The consul rejoicing in the augury and the presence of the gods, ordered a blare of trumpets and a cheer !

Livy says of this same Papirius that never did a general seem more joyful in battle than he did, either from his own genius or his confidence in success.   In the climax of the battle, a time when temples are vowed to the gods, he vowed to Jupiter the Victor that if he had routed the le-

[89] 5, 22.   [90] 10, 40 and 42.

gions of the enemy, he would offer a wine-glass of mead to
Jupiter before he himself quaffed a beaker of stout !   The
gods liked the vow and made the auspices good.   Direct
speech, supreme self-confidence, jovial spirits, the glow of
victory enliven these stories of how Papirius kept the gods
on his side.

As Livy's history progresses there appear in the second
century B.C., two movements : an official attempt to check
the multiplication of prodigies ; an equally official effort to
protect the old religion against the invasion of new cults.
In the year 193 B.C., so many earthquakes were reported
that men grew tired of the facts and of the holidays proclaimed on account of them, for the senate could not meet
and affairs of state could not be transacted while the consuls were occupied in sacrifices and expiatory rites. Finally
the consuls on the authority of the senate, announced that
after one earthquake had been reported and proper rites
ordained, no other earthquake could be reported on that
day.[91]   Here was clearly, to use our modern phraseology,
a sort of compromise between church and state.

At a time when a more serious menace to the government was involved, senate and consuls took entire responsibility for restrictive measures.   An instance is the
suppression of the Bacchanalian conspiracy in 186 B.C.[92]
The art of this remarkable story will be discussed under
anecdotes about women.   Here we must note only that
the secret rites of Bacchus were reported to be a source of
corruption to the young of both sexes ; that thousands
were involved in them ; and that because of the numbers
attending the meetings of the cult, the state feared a political conspiracy and decreed strongly repressive measures.
These broke up official organization of the cult as no common treasury was allowed, no director of sacrifices, no

[91] 34, 55.   [92] 39, 8–19 ; *C. I. L.* I. 196.

priest.   Religious freedom was respected by special per-
missions, granted by the city praetor and the senate, to
devout votaries to make sacrifices when not more than five
persons took part in the rite.

A few years later, 181 B.C., the burning of "the Books
of Numa" was an official act against the subversion of the
old religion.[93]   At the foot of the Janiculum on the land
of Lucius Petilius, a public clerk, when farmers were digging, two stone chests sealed with lead were discovered.
Each had an inscription in Latin and Greek, one stating
that here Numa Pompilius was buried, the other that the
Books of Numa were within.   The sepulchre of Numa
was empty, but in the other chest were two bundles, one
containing seven Latin books on pontifical law, one seven
Greek books of a philosophical cult, called by some authorities Pythagorean.   The friends of Petilius read them,
then many others, then the praetor, Quintus Petilius.   He
found them subversive of religion and said they should
be burned, but he gave the clerk an opportunity to seek
legal advice about his rights of possession.   Through the
tribunes, Lucius appealed to the senate.   On the advice
of the praetor, the senate decreed that the Books should
be burned but adequate compensation should be given
to Lucius Petilius.   This he refused.   The Books were
burned in the comitium in the sight of the people.   It is
notable that no religious advice was taken about the con-
tents of the Books.

In the same century there is a conspicuous instance of
science combating superstition.[94]   In 168 B.C., in the war
with the Macedonians a military tribune, Gaius Sulpicius
Gallus, with the consul's permission, assembled his soldiers
and explained to them an eclipse of the moon which was to
occur on the following night, that they might not consider

[93] 40, 29.   [94] 44, 37.

it a portent.   When the moon disappeared according to Gallus' forecast, the Roman soldiers thought his learning almost divine.[95]   The Macedonians believed that the eclipse was an evil portent predicting the downfall of their kingdom and the destruction of their nation so they shouted and wailed until the moon reappeared.

These various anecdotes have been selected to show how humor creeps into stories of *religio,* then fear of political complications in new cults or subversion of old worship, and finally the beginning of a public, scientific attitude towards natural phenomena.

In short, crisp narratives often enlivened by conversation Livy shows the tremendous part which *religio* played in the Roman state and the varying attitudes towards it. Scattered amid these records are direct statements and comments which reveal Livy's own point of view of the need of *religio* in the state, its dangers and its blessings. In the preface, the author states that he includes in his

[95] "There can be little doubt that the total eclipse of the moon cited by Livy in *ab Urbe Condita*, 44, 37, as taking place on the night before the nones of September in 168 B.C. from the second to the fourth hour, actually occurred on the night of June 21st. The only other lunar eclipse of that year took place on December 16 and the text explicitly refers in a preceding paragraph to the passing of the summer solstice and to the intense heat and drought of the season.

The circumstances of the two eclipses are given below for the purpose of comparison.   It will be noted that in both cases the moon had entered the umbra and the partial phase had begun before the moon appeared above the horizon.

date	168 B.C.	June 21	Dec. 16
approx. local time of sunset and moonrise		7.35	4.25 P.M.
moon enters umbra and partial phase begins		6.42	4.08
moon immersed in umbra, totality begins		7.52	5.13
middle of eclipse		8.28	5.57
moon begins to emerge, totality ends		9.04	6.41
partial phase ends		10.14	7.46

Data for the computation were taken from Oppolzer, Canon der Finsternisse, Vienna, 1887, page 340, for eclipses numbered 1596 and 1597. The time is local apparent time; the latitude was taken as 41° north and the longitude as 23° east of Greenwich, for Macedon." Note prepared by Maud W. Makemson, June 17, 1939.

work the myths of the origins of Rome because they add
an aura of sanctity, and he invokes the blessings of the
gods on his history.   Yet he recognizes the danger of superstitious awe, for several times he records the fact that in
time of panic more omens and portents were reported,
superstition increased, strange rites were introduced and
many soothsayers were making gain out of men's fears.[96]
In spite of this menace, he regrets the contemporary neglect
of religion, saying of the early republic :

> There had not yet come about that contempt for the gods which
> possesses the present generation ; nor did everybody seek to con-
> strue oaths and laws to suit himself, but rather shaped his own
> practices by them.[97]

Much later in his history in a very significant passage
he states fully his reasons for giving so much space in his
libri to the phenomena of religion : [98]

> I am aware that because of the same negligence on account of
> which men now believe that the gods send no portents, no prod-
> igies at this time are announced to the state or recorded in its
> annals.   But as I write of ancient history somehow my spirit be-
> comes ancient and a certain religious awe compels me to regard
> those portents which the wise men of old decreed should be ap-
> peased by the state as worthy of a place in my history.

This avowed sympathy with the ancient religion is what
made Livy compose the dramatic speech for Camillus
against deserting Rome for Veii.[99]   The whole oration is
filled with horror at the thought of abandoning a city
founded by auspices and augury, filled with religious as-
sociations and the presence of the gods.   And as the general appealed to the Romans to protect the Capitol, the fires
of Vesta, the shields from heaven, an omen approved his

---

[96] 3, 5–6 ; 22, 1 ; 25, 1 ; 27, 37 ; 28, 11 ; 29, 14 ; 41, 16.
[97] 3, 20, translated by B. O. Foster in *The Loeb Classical Library.*
[98] 43, 13.   [99] 5, 50–55.

eloquence, for a chance word of a centurion on guard duty
was heard by the senate in deliberation : "Standard-bearer
set up the standard.   Here 'tis best to stay."

These anecdotes of religion are of course interwoven
with stories of women, since from the earliest times women
were priestesses in Rome and both *pietas* and *castitas* were
virtues directly under the approval of the gods.   Livy has
numerous stories of Vestals who were true to their vows
and of Vestals who were false.   There are also stories of noble ladies who were chaste and reverent and of high-born
women who through love of power stooped to crime.
All these types of stories are forecast in early myths of
Rome which have become famous.   The very mention of
their heroines recalls the telling : Tarpeia, the Vestal, who
was false or true according to your interpretation of her
un-arming of the Sabines ; [100] Lucretia with her dagger
pouring out her blood to prove that in spite of rape her
spirit was pure ; [101] the maid, Verginia, slain with a butch-
er's knife by her own father to protect her from a noble's
lust ; [102] the aged Veturia, mother of Coriolanus, standing
with his wife and small sons, persuading the great exile to
withdraw his army from besieging Rome ; [103] the terrible
murderess, Tullia, bespattered with her own father's royal
blood.[104]   Here are *bona* and *mala exempla* of Rome's
family traditions and horrors.

The Vestal Virgins, priestesses of the goddess of the
hearth, were held in the greatest reverence from the time
of Romulus.   When the Gauls were about to sack Rome,
and the Vestals were carrying their sacred objects from the
city, a plebeian, Lucius Albinius, on seeing them, made his
wife and children dismount from the wagon in which he
was conveying them to safety, and instead drove the Vestals

[100] 1, 11.   [103] 2, 40.
[101] 1, 57–60.   [104] 1, 46–48.
[102] 3, 44–51, 56–58.

and their burdens to Caere.[105]   Such respect and honor demanded that no breath of scandal should ever touch their fame.   In 420 B.C., a Vestal named Postumia was tried on the charge of unchastity because her elegant clothes and merry tongue aroused suspicion.   She was acquitted, but the pontifex maximus ordered her in future to abstain from jokes and to dress in a religious rather than an elegant style.[106]   The Vestal Minucia who was also talked about because of her elegance was convicted on the evidence of a slave and buried alive near the Colline Gate.[107]   In the midst of the alarms of war and the people's belief that the gods were angry because of many portents, the Vestal Oppia was found to have offended them by breaking her vow of chastity and was executed.[108]   Also in the panic of war time a Vestal was flogged to death because the fire in the temple of Vesta had gone out in her watch.[109]   In the first Punic War, among other portents, two Vestals, Opimia and Floronia, were convicted of unchastity.   One was buried alive near the Colline Gate, the other committed suicide.   Lucius Cantilius, a secretary of the pontiffs, the lover of Floronia, was flogged to death. Such was the religious horror at this pollution that human sacrifice was actually decreed by the Sibylline Books.   And the sacrifice, as if in expiation of sex sins, was of two couples, a Gaulish man and woman, a Greek man and woman, who were all buried alive in the Forum Boarium, a sacrifice, Livy comments, by no means Roman.[110]   Rarely was a Vestal accused of unchastity able to prove her innocence through divine aid, but Claudia Quintia did.   For suspicion of her was removed when the Great Mother, Cybele, allowed Claudia to escort her symbol, the Black

[105] 5, 40.
[106] 4, 44.
[107] 8, 15.

[108] 2, 42.
[109] 28, 11.
[110] 22, 57.

Stone, in safety to Rome.[111]   These stories of Vestals are
not told elaborately, indeed are hardly more than brief
mentions, but there is one very interesting fact about them.
That is the author's hint implicit in the context that the
condemnation of several for unchastity and their execution
were due to war panic which wished to appease angry gods.

Several stories about women are concerned with social
status and arose from the political struggles between patricians and plebeians over the equalization of the orders.
The scene of one is the little town of Ardea where the
episode caused civil war.[112]   A girl of plebeian rank, famous for her beauty, had two suitors, one of her own rank
favored by her plebeian guardians, the other a noble, supported by leaders of society and favored by the girl's mother
who was ambitious to have her daughter make a grand
match.   Since the girl's mother and guardians could not
agree, the matter was taken to court.   There the magistrate ruled that the mother should have the right of decision.   The indignant guardians with a band of plebeians
then kidnapped the girl, but they were met by an enraged
band of young nobles and a desperate battle followed.   So
civil war started, Livy comments, from the mad passion of
two young men who sought a fatal marriage which involved the ruin of their country.   From this point the
anecdote changes from a love-story to a narrative of war
between Romans and Volscians who were summoned by
the two factions in Ardea to their aid.   We never hear
what became of the girl nor do we know her name.

In Rome itself, social rivalry between two sisters is assigned by Livy as one of the potent factors in the final
equalization of the orders.[113]   In 377 B.C., the fortunes

[111] 29, 11 and 14 ; Ovid, *Fasti,* 4,
247–325 ; Tac. *Ann.* 4, 64. Livy
makes Claudia a Roman matron, not
a Vestal.

[112] 4, 9–11.
[113] 6, 34–42.

of the plebeians were at their lowest ebb because of the terrible laws against debtors.   The poverty-stricken plebeians no longer presented candidates for their own magistracies, the tribuneships.   An influential noble named Marcus Fabius Ambustus was very popular with the plebs because of his known sympathy and because while he had married his elder daughter to Servius Sulpicius, he had married his younger to an able young plebeian, named Gaius Licinius Stolo.   So much social etiquette, feminine psychology and fatherly sympathy are involved in the narrative which follows that I am going to quote Livy's paragraph.[114]

It fell out that the sisters Fabia were together in the house of Servius Sulpicius, then a consular tribune, and were whiling away the time in talk, as women will, when a lictor of Sulpicius, who was returning from the Forum, rapped on the door, in the usual manner, with his rod.   At this the younger Fabia, being unused to the custom, went white, which made the elder laugh with surprise at her sister's ignorance.   But that laugh rankled in the other's mind, for a woman's feelings are influenced by trifles.   I suppose, too, that the crowd of people who attended the tribune and took a ceremonious leave of him made her look upon her sister's marriage as a fortunate one and regret her own, in that ill-judging spirit which makes us all so very loath to be outdone by our nearest friends.

She was still suffering from the smart of wounded pride, when her father, happening to see her, asked if anything was wrong. She would fain have concealed the reason of her grief, which was too little consistent with sisterly affection and did no great honour to her husband ; but he brought her by tender inquiries to confess that she was unhappy in being mated to one beneath her, having married into a house where neither dignities nor influence could enter.   Ambustus then comforted his daughter and bade her be of good cheer : she would see ere long in her own home the same state she beheld at her sister's.   From that moment he began to make plans with his son-in-law, taking into their counsels also Lucius Sextius, a strenuous youth, whose aspirations were thwarted only by his lack of patrician blood.

[114] 6, 34, translated by B. O. Foster in *The Loeb Classical Library.*

The results of the younger Fabia's jealousy of her sister's social prestige were that her husband, Licinius, and Sextius were elected plebeian tribunes ten times in successive years ; in their tenth year of office they got a law passed requiring that half of the decemvirs in charge of the sacred rites must be plebeian and finally in 367 B.C., that one of the consuls should be plebeian and to this office Lucius Sextius was elected. The younger Fabia has disappeared from the story, but she must have been gratified by the long and successful political career of her husband, Licinius. Perhaps she remembered her father's consoling reassurances when she was a sensitive young bride.

An amusing story about the privileges of parents in high life is told by Livy of Scipio Africanus.[115]   It came from the time when in the absence of Scipio Africanus, his brother Lucius was arraigned for investigation of the money taken from King Antiochus and an enormous fine imposed upon him on suspicion that he had not delivered over to the state all the King's wealth. The praetor, Tiberius Gracchus, a political enemy of the Scipios, imposed the fine but declared that he would not permit so great a Roman general to be thrown into that prison to which his brother Africanus had conducted so many kings and commanders of the enemy.

The story goes on that the senate, which chanced to dine that day on the Capitoline, had risen up and begged that during the banquet Africanus should betroth his daughter to Gracchus. When the contract had been duly made at this public ceremony and Scipio had returned home, he told his wife Aemilia that he had arranged a marriage for their younger daughter.   When she, being irritated, as a woman would naturally be, that he had not consulted with her about the daughter of both of them, had added that not even if he were promising her to Tiberius Gracchus should the mother have been excluded from the deliberation,

[115] 38, 57 and 60.

Scipio, they say, rejoicing at their harmony of opinion, replied that it was to Gracchus that he had betrothed her.[116]

The pride of Aemilia, her insistence on a mother's right of being consulted about the betrothal of her daughter and Scipio's adroit reconciliation make this a delicious episode in the stormy careers of the Scipios.

The story of the repeal of the Oppian Law in 195 B.C., is one of the most elaborate pictures extant of the position of women in the Roman republic.[117]   This law which had been passed in the height of the first Punic war decreed that no woman should possess more than half an ounce of gold, wear a robe of different colors, or ride in a carriage in Rome or in a town within a mile of it except at the time of religious celebrations.   Now that the war was over, two tribunes of the plebs proposed in the interest of the women the abrogation of the law.   Many famous men spoke for and against the repeal.   And the matrons could not be kept at home by authority or modesty or the commands of their husbands, but they filled all the streets and the approaches to the Forum and argued with the men as they entered it.   The situation is presented by Livy in two quoted speeches, one by Marcus Porcius Cato against repeal, the other by the tribune, Lucius Valerius, in behalf of the bill which he had proposed.   Both speeches are closely knit, eloquent, in character with the speaker, and rich in revelation of the position of women at the time.

Cato argued in brief : "Because we have not controlled our individual wives, we are afraid of these assembled women.   Are laws to be accepted because of a secession of ladies ?   What is this custom of running out into the streets, picketing, haranguing the husbands of others ?   I

[116] 38, 57, translated by Evan T. Sage in *The Loeb Classical Library*.
[117] 34, 1–8.

tell you, these women are aiming at complete liberty ! And as soon as they begin to be our equals, they will be our superiors.

"The two vices of the state are avarice and luxury.   You are starting a contest for display among your wives.   Worst of all, they are demanding a law and votes and they are securing them from some men."

Valerius defended the measure by first attacking Cato's words "a sedition," "a secession of women" and their savage untruth.   Then he read from Cato's own *Origines* previous instances of women appearing in public in the war with the Sabines, in their appeal to Coriolanus.   He continued : "Why should we not listen to their appeal ? Our ears are too proud if, although as masters we do not refuse to listen to the petitions of slaves, we scorn appeals from honorable ladies.

"Moreover, the Oppian Law was a war measure and should be repealed in peace.   It was passed only twenty years ago and before it our matrons lived virtuously and without extravagance.   Our wives should enjoy the rewards of peace and some elegance.

"They are not asking for liberty : they always deplore the liberty which loss of husbands and fathers creates.   Of course, you should keep them under control and guardianship, but not in slavery.   You should prefer to be called fathers and husbands to masters.

"There is no danger of a secession of women like that of the plebeians.   Whatever you decree, the frailer sex must endure.   Therefore the more power you have the more moderately you should use it."

With these reassuring statements Valerius achieved the passing of the repeal !

A strange episode of sex warfare is on record in the

earlier history of Rome.   If Cato knew it, it substantiated
all his fears of women's power.[118]   Livy is very doubtful
about its authenticity, but says he must tell the story as it
came to him.   When the leading men of the state were
falling sick with the same illness which was generally fatal,
a maid-servant went to the curule aedile, Quintus Fabius
Maximus, and declared that she would testify to the cause
of the epidemic if she were assured protection after her
testimony.   When the aedile and the senate gave her the
desired assurance, she revealed a plot of the women in the
state for wholesale poisoning.   She declared, moreover,
that she could lead them at once to the places where the
poisons were being brewed.   By her aid twenty matrons
were caught in the act and arrested.   Two patricians,
Cornelia and Sergia, declared that the drugs were medici-
nal.   The informer asserting that they lied asked them to
drink the concoctions to attest their veracity.   The two
ladies after conference with the other prisoners announced
that they would drink their brews.   On doing so all twenty
died.   Their attendants were seized and informed against
a large number of matrons, and one hundred and seventy
were found guilty.

Since up to that time there had never been a trial for
poisoning in Rome, many regarded this episode as a portent and believed the women insane rather than criminal.
So an old custom of appointing a dictator to drive a nail
as an expiatory rite was revived, for by that ceremony men's
minds had of old been brought back to sanity.   This is a
brief, exciting narrative of what Livy calls a year made
terrible either by bad weather or the wickedness of mankind.

Another crime wave, in this case linked with religion,
has already been referred to under the name of the Bac-

118 8, 18.

chanalian conspiracy.[119]   The events took place in 186 B.C.
The *senatus consultum* which suppressed the Bacchanalia
is extant.[120]   Livy's story is unusually long and contains
an unusual number of characters who are mentioned by
name.   It is a serious record of an episode which involves
Roman conservatism in religion, tenacity of moral standards, respect for youth and fear of subversive powers in
politics and morality.

Livy gave first an account of how a nameless Greek introduced the rites of Bacchus into Etruria whence they
spread to Rome.   Then he explained their nature : they
were nocturnal, secret, celebrated with wine and banquets
by both sexes, orgies in which every kind of lust was satisfied ; they involved debauchery, poisonings and murders,
but the cries of the victims were concealed by the howlings
of the votaries, the clash of cymbals, the beating of drums.

The iniquities involved became known in Rome
through their menace to a young knight named Publius
Aebutius.   His father and his guardians had died so he
was being brought up by his mother, Duronia, and his
stepfather, Titus Sempronius Rutilus.   His stepfather had
mismanaged his ward's property so that he could not give
an account of the funds.   Therefore he wished to get rid
of the young man or get him in his power so that he would
not present charges.   A sure way of corruption was the
Bacchanalia.   Aebutius' mother told her son that when he
was ill, she had made a vow that as soon as he recovered
she would initiate him into the rites of Bacchus ; that the
time for the fulfillment of the vow had come ; he must
therefore lead a chaste life for ten days ; on the tenth after
a banquet and a ceremonial bath she would lead him to
the sanctuary.

Young Aebutius was devoted to a famous courtesan, a

[119] 39, 8–19.   [120] *C.I.L.* I. 196.

freedwoman named Hispala Faecenia.   Her patron had
died.   She had fallen in love with Aebutius and since his
relatives were stingy about his allowance, she supported
him generously and had made him her sole heir.   Aebutius returned her devotion and since they had no secrets
from each other, he told her as a joke that she must not be
surprised at his absence for several nights : to satisfy a vow
he was going to be initiated in the rites of Bacchus.   Hispala full of consternation cried : "The gods forbid !" and
declared that he and she might better die than have this
happen and she called down curses on those who had persuaded him to this action.   Aebutius told her not to be
alarmed, for they were his mother and his stepfather.
"Then," cried Hispala, "your stepfather — for perhaps it
is wrong to accuse your mother — is hastening by this act
to destroy your virtue, your reputation, your prospects,
and your life."

To meet her lover's amazement, she then told him that
as a slave she had once accompanied her mistress to that
shrine (she had never visited it as a freedwoman) and she
described graphically the terrible corruption and debauchery that went on there.   Finally she exacted a promise
from him that he would never be initiated in these mysteries.

When Aebutius went home and told this decision to his
mother and stepfather, in great anger they drove him out
of the house.   He went to his aunt, Aebutia, and told
her the whole story.   On her advice the next day he reported the matter to the consul, Postumius, in a private
interview.   The consul made investigations through his
mother-in-law, Sulpicia, who attested Aebutia's noble character and brought her to her own home for a secret interview with the consul.   After Postumius heard her story,
he had his mother-in-law summon also Hispala.   She,

alarmed by the consul's presence and realizing that Aebutius had betrayed her information, could hardly be persuaded to speak for terror, but finally when assurances of protection were given her, she gave a full account of the origin of the mysteries, their development and their orgies. The consul protected her by persuading his mother-in-law to give her an apartment in her house. He moved Aebutius at once to the house of a client of his. Thus having secured his witnesses, he proceeded to efficient plans for the suppression of the Bacchanalia. He presented an official report to the senate which passed a decree in support of his work ; then he held a meeting of the people at which he made a long speech. This oration by its black picture of the Bacchanalian orgies, by its reports of the numbers involved in them was skillfully directed to lead the people to fear of a conspiracy arising from secret, nocturnal meetings of such proportions. And he urged that though the crimes of the votaries had been private so far, the real aim of the cult was control of the state. It was therefore against a conspiracy that repressive measures were to be taken.

So informers were encouraged and arrests began. Seven thousand men and women were said to be involved. Many fled. Many were imprisoned. Many were executed. The Bacchanalia were forbidden. Suitable rewards for information were given to Publius Aebutius and Hispala Faecenia. Protection for life was insured to Hispala and she was permitted to marry whomever she wished, even a man of free birth. It was decreed that no fraud or disgrace should attach to the husband of her choice. Livy does not tell us whether she and Aebutius married ! In this story Livy does not introduce personal comment except in saying that Hispala was worthy of a better profession than the one she practised. Yet implicit in the

narrative is the opinion that a "conspiracy" was not proven,
but the religious rites were suppressed because of fear of
growing numbers of votaries whose secret assemblies might
be diverted from worship to revolution.   This latent psychology as well as the clear drawing of the characters involved intensify the interest of the story.   It is told with
varied technique : narrative, dialogue, oration.   The account of the immorality of the rites is told three times :
in the introductory narrative by the author as a simple
statement of fact, by Hispala to her lover in impassioned
terror for him, by Hispala to the consul Postumius under
compulsion and after assurance of protection.   This last
account is by far the longest and most detailed, is indeed
the climax of the whole story as its veracity moves the
consul to report the matter to the senate and achieve the
repression of the rites.

There are many other significant stories of women in
Livy's history : of other courtesans who served the state,[121]
of foreign ladies who played heroic parts,[122] of one Apulian
woman who fed thousands of refugee Roman soldiers.[123]
The most famous story of a foreign woman is the love-story
of Sophonisba, daughter of Hasdrubal, and Masinissa, the
Numidian prince.[124]   No other story in Livy except perhaps the rape of Lucretia has had such great influence in
later literature.   The stories which I have selected out of
all this rich material are ones especially significant for
social, religious, and political life in Rome.

Certain anecdotes in Livy are concerned wholly with
politics.   As in the other types, these begin with myths :
the murder of Remus in the rivalry of two brothers for
the founding of Rome,[125] the disappearance of Romulus

[121] 26, 12.
[122] 24, 22–25, 38, 24 ; 40, 3–4.
[123] 22, 52 and 54.

[124] 29, 23 and 30, 12–15. See E. H.
Haight, *Essays on Ancient Fiction*,
New York, 1936, pp. 30–33.
[125] 1, 7.

by deification or murder,[126] "the peaceable penetration" by which the Etruscan Lucumo made himself overlord of Rome, and so King Tarquin.[127]   There are terrible instances of a father's exercise of the *patria potestas* in the execution of a son in the cases of Brutus, of Aulus Postumius, of Titus Manlius.[128]   But two types of political anecdotes are more significant than all the others : stories about the condition of debtors and stories about careers that were ruined because of suspected ambition for excessive power.

In the year 495 B.C., the state was torn by bitter dissensions between the patricians and the plebeians because of the tragic condition of men who had been bound out to service because of their debts.   Men who had fought for the liberty of their country had been taken prisoners by their fellow-citizens.   A conspicuous instance nearly fanned the smoldering class hatred into the flame of war.[129] An aged man, the personification of misfortune, rushed into the Forum.   He was poorly dressed, dirty, pale, emaciated.   His unkempt hair and beard made him look like a savage.   Nevertheless he was recognized as a former army officer and he himself bared his breast to show his scars.   To inquiries about his condition he related that while he was serving in the Sabine War, the enemy had devastated his farm, burned his house, plundered everything, driven away his flocks.   At this dreadful time taxes were imposed on him, he had contracted debts, interest on them swelled, he had lost the farm owned by his father and grandfather, then all the rest of his property, and finally his own person, for he had been carried off by his creditor not to slavery, but to prison and torture.   As proof he showed on his back the welts of recent scourgings.

[126] 1, 16.
[127] 1, 34-35.
[128] 2, 5 ; 4, 29 ; 8, 7.
[129] 2, 23-24.

This sight and his speech so inflamed the people that a mob gathered and demanded that the senate meet to right their wrongs. The consuls for a long time could not assemble the senate because of the terror of the members. The crowd grew more clamorous. At last a sufficient number of senators for a meeting collected, but the opinions of the members about measures to be taken were divided.

At this crisis an enemy, the Volscians, were reported to be advancing on the city. In this war emergency, the consul, Servilius, adjourned the senate and went before the people. He declared that the senators had every intention of taking measures to relieve their situation but now all Rome must unite to meet the enemy. He therefore proclaimed that during the war no one could hold in chains a Roman citizen who might enlist and while he was in military service, no one could seize his property or annoy his children or his grandchildren. The debtors volunteered in throngs.

Of course, this relief was only temporary. A hundred years later history repeated itself.[130] This is a long story which involves the career of Marcus Manlius who had saved the Capitol from the Gauls. In the year 385 B.C., Manlius saw in the middle of the Forum a centurion, famous for military exploits, condemned for debt and being led away as a captive. Manlius with his escort forced his way to the creditor, paid the sufferer's debts in the sight of all the people and set him free. Later he inflamed the people still more by selling a farm, the main part of his property, so that he might have more money in hand to ransom debtors. It was again a time of war with the Volscians and a dictator was appointed. The dictator feared a popular revolution at home led by Manlius. Manlius

[130] 6, 11–20.

was therefore brought to trial, but Livy says he finds no record of any evidence against him of aiming at royal power, except his generosity to debtors and his speeches to meetings of the plebs. Nevertheless he was condemned and thrown down from the Tarpeian Rock, from the Capitol which he had saved. The dramatic story is told at length by vivid descriptions, many direct speeches, prayers, Livy's personal comments, and an implicit sense of the irony of destiny.

The end of the debtors' wrongs did not come until the year 326 B.C. Then it was brought about by the tragedy of a young boy.[131] Gaius Publilius had given himself up for a debt contracted by his father to Lucius Papirius. The boy's youth and beauty fired in the heart of the creditor not pity, but lust. When Papirius could not corrupt the lad by lewd talk and proposals or by threats, he had him stripped and flogged. The mangled lad rushed out on the streets complaining of the lust and cruelty of the money-lender. A great crowd of people, moved by pity and indignation and by the thought of their own children, assembled, forced a meeting of the senate and as each senator arrived, displayed to him the boy's lacerated back. That day the liberty of the plebs had a new beginning, for no longer could men be imprisoned for debt. This is impassioned brief narrative completed in a single chapter.

In the long struggle between the patricians and plebeians in the early republic, Manlius was not the only one who lost his life because of his aid to the poor. After the expulsion of the kings, the Romans were so sensitive about their liberty that one of the first consuls, Valerius Maximus, had to move the new house he was building down from an eminence on the Velia because its first lofty site was suspected of being a citadel from which he could storm

131 8, 28.

the city and make himself king.[132]   Spurius Maelius, a
plebeian, because of his free distribution of grain to the
people was suspected of aiming at kingship by plotting
revolution and bribing the tribunes to betray liberty and
was murdered.[133]   Careers of nobles too were ruined in
these violent struggles between the classes.   A dashing
young swashbuckler of a noble, Caeso Quinctius, who with
his followers often drove the tribunes from the Forum and
routed the plebs with their officials, was driven into exile
(perhaps killed) on the evidence of one of the tribunes,
which was afterwards suspected of having been falsified.[134]
Another episode Livy relates, he says, though it is unim-
portant in itself, as an illustration of the plebeians' struggle for their liberty.   Gnaeus Flavius, a government clerk,
had been elected curule aedile to the great disgust of the
patricians.   Once when he went to call on a sick colleague,
the young nobles who were present did not rise on his en-
trance.   Flavius ordered his curule chair brought in and
taking his seat on it stared calmly at the rude young aristocrats.[135]   This anecdote is an anticlimax to the long,
thrilling stories of the ruin of Maelius and of Caeso but,
as Livy claimed, it has a great point.   The liberty of the
plebs no less than the liberty of the whole Roman state
was a keynote of these class struggles of the fifth and fourth
centuries.   Livy in his narratives shows fairness and understanding of this second great contest for liberty in the
Roman world and makes the final victory of the plebs seem
no less important for *libertas* than the expulsion of the
kings.

The backbone of Livy's whole history consists of stories
of war.   There are multitudinous war anecdotes and many
serial stories of varying length.   Some are colored by

[132] 2, 7.
[133] 4, 13–16, 21.
[134] 3, 11–14, 19, 25.
[135] 9, 46.

propaganda for the state.   The majority are told in heroic
outlines to make war magnificent.   Through this splendor, however, there are unshed *lacrimae rerum* and pictures of war's horrors painted with stark realism evoke pity
and terror.

The early stories are epic and unforgettable : the conflict of the Horatii and the Curiatii,[136] Horatius holding
the bridge,[137] Curtius on his horse leaping into the chasm
in the Forum.[138]   In historical times too, many single episodes are told with the same poignancy as the myths.   A
Decius "devotes" himself in battle as a sacrifice to the gods
of the lower world to insure victory.[139]   A consul casts his
standard into the enemy's stockade to make his men charge
after it.[140]   The Romans tunneling under the citadel of
Veii dash out and steal the vital organs of a victim because
they hear a soothsayer announce that whoever carves these
organs will bring success to his people.[141]

There are vignettes of strange types of battle.   Before
Fidenae, in the war of the Romans against the Fidenates
and the Etruscans, men fought with fire instead of weapons.[142]   For out of the gates of the besieged city the enemy
rushed waving flaming firebrands, and the dictator, Quinctius, had to rally his soldiers by shouting : "Are you to be
smoked out like a swarm of bees by your foes ?   Will you
not seize their torches and turn their own weapons upon
the city of the enemy ?"   In a war with the Volscians, 423
B.C., the fight on the little mound became famous in history.[143]   The war was going against the Romans, for the
consul, Sempronius, was no general, and retreat was im-
minent.   That disgrace was averted by a centurion of the
cavalry, Sextus Tempanius, for he shouted that the horse-

[136] 1, 24–26.
[137] 2, 10.
[138] 7, 6.
[139] 8, 9–11 ; 10, 28.
[140] 4, 29.
[141] 5, 21.
[142] 4, 31–34.
[143] 4, 38–41.

men who wished to save their country should dismount, and when his troops obeyed, he called : "Unless this bucklered cohort halts the onset of the enemy, the state is overthrown. Follow my lance as a standard. Show the Romans and the Volscians that when you are horsemen, no horsemen equal you, when you are infantry, no infantry equal you." The cohort followed Tempanius' lance into the thick of the battle wherever they saw their friends most beset. So valiant was their fighting that the Volscian general ordered that a way should be opened for the new cohort and by that strategy he surrounded them. Tempanius and his men took a little mound and on it standing in a circle fought. They were ringed about by the Volscians who had to fight in two directions, against them and the Romans who were trying to relieve them. Only night halted the uncertain struggle and both armies in terror of each other led their forces to the hills. At earliest dawn Tempanius moved his troops down from the mound, and finding the camps of both Romans and Volscians deserted, marched his men safely back to Rome.

There one of the plebeian tribunes brought charges against the consul, Sempronius, for inefficiency and tried to force Tempanius to bear witness against him. But Tempanius replied in a speech that was crude but full of a soldier's honor, for he did not praise himself or attack his general, but swore that the consul had done all he could to save the army and that fate and the dark had made victory impossible. The wounded hero was dismissed with as much praise for his moderation as for his valor.

There are many anecdotes of individual courage as duels are fought in which heroes shine. Titus Manlius accepted the challenge of a giant Gaul who had stuck out his tongue at the Roman in derision before fighting, fatally stabbed him below the waist, and from the torque which

he took from his fallen foe won the name Torquatus.[144]
Marcus Valerius fought a duel with another huge Gaul
and was assisted by the gods to victory, for a raven alighted
on his helmet and whenever the two closed in, attacked the
face and eyes of the Gaul, until his terror brought about
his death and Valerius won the name of Corvus.[145]   In another episode two horsemen, Roman and Campanian, after
a prelude of furious words, fought, dismounted, remounted
and parted when the Campanian showed the white flag of
cowardice.[146]   Again a Campanian and a Roman who had
been guest friends met in true Homeric style with a long
battle of words before the actual combat and fought until
the Campanian, dismounted and wounded, ran off to his
friends.[147]   These are but a few specimens of the diverse
and picturesque anecdotes of warfare.

Besides these there are long narratives of foreign wars
which might be lifted from Livy's *libri* and published
as separate monographs.   These are the invasion of the
Gauls,[148] the Punic Wars,[149] and the rivalry of the sons
of Perseus.[150]   They are all vital parts of the history of
Rome, but each is complete in itself, and each illustrates
fully Livy's remarkable art of narration.   The limited
scope of this essay does not permit a study of their elaborate technique or of the interweaving of anecdotes in the
framework of each whole.   The three illustrate what Cicero had in mind in the letter which begged Lucceius to
incorporate a study of the conspiracy of Catiline in his
history.[151]   In each the rise and fall of a great nation (the
Gauls) or of a great leader (Hannibal, Perseus) makes
Livy's story as tragic in coloring as Greek drama so that the

[144] 7, 9–10.
[145] 7, 26.
[146] 23, 47
[147] 25, 18.
[148] 5, 32–50.

[149] Books 21–26.   Also 33, 48 ; 35,
14 ; 39, 51.
[150] 40, 5–16, 20–24, 54–57.
[151] Cic. *ad Fam.* V. 12.   See pp.
41–42.

sight of how the high are brought low arouses the emotions of pity and fear.

But not all Livy's war stories strut the stage in tragic robes. He describes betrayals, massacres, mass suicides, gory defeats with a stark reality that produces an instantaneous reaction of shuddering horror and dispels all glamour. Tales of treason picture incredible villainy on the part of friends. When Romans and Carthaginians were vying for the allegiance of southern Italy in 212 B.C., the Lucanian Flavus, seeking to ingratiate himself with the Carthaginians, deceived the Roman general, Gracchus, by a plausible story of a secret meeting of the praetors of all the Lucanian states who were now ready to support the Romans, led him with a small escort into a wooded mountain valley and there had the whole band slaughtered.[152]

In the same war in 214 B.C., the lofty citadel of Henna, the sacred seat of the cult of Ceres and Proserpina, was the scene of a terrible betrayal and massacre.[153] The Roman governor, Lucius Pinarius, refused to surrender his garrison to the Carthaginians at the request of the leading citizens of the town, and knowing how other cities had been betrayed to the enemy assembled his soldiers, revealed to them the situation and told them that by the next night Henna would be drenched with their blood or the blood of the inhabitants. The next day he called an assembly of the people in the theater. All exits from the city had been closed by his soldiers. When he argued against giving over the keys of the city to the Carthaginians and the people in anger threatened him madly, he gave the signal agreed on and his soldiers closed in on the assembly. All the inhabitants of Henna were put to death by the sword, even the unarmed. "So Henna," comments

[152] 25, 16.   [153] 24, 37-39.

Livy, "was retained by a terrible deed that was either wicked or necessary."

The despair of war caused not only massacre, but wholesale suicides. Capua which had deserted the Roman cause for Hannibal was being besieged in 211 B.C., and no relief came. The messengers whom they sent with a letter of appeal to Hannibal and the spies sent into the Roman army were all apprehended by the Romans, flogged and sent back into Capua with their hands cut off. Their terrible plight proved to the Capuans that the end was near so twenty-seven senators inspired by Vibius Virius committed suicide by taking poison.[154] In the little town of Astapa in Spain self-immolation was more complete, for the inhabitants first piled a huge bonfire in the forum with their possessions, their wives and children placed on it, and a guard of fifty young men about it to fire it if the day was lost ; then they rushed out into open battle and fought till the last man died. Whereupon the guard of fifty youths in Astapa set fire to the pile, watched the women and children burn, and at last jumped into the flames.[155]

Defeat could be faced by the Romans with fortitude and a dogged resolution to carry on. After the disaster at Lake Trasimene the praetor announced to Rome the calamity in a simple sentence : "We have been conquered in a great battle." [156] But Livy does not spare his readers the horrors of defeat. There is no more ghastly war-picture than his description of the battle-field after Cannae.[157]

The morning after, as soon as it was light, they pressed forward to collect the spoil and to gaze on a carnage that was ghastly even to enemies. There lay those thousands upon thousands of Ro-

[154] 26, 14–15.
[155] 28, 22–23.
[156] 22, 7.

[157] 22, 51, translated by B. O. Foster in *The Loeb Classical Library.*

mans, foot and horse indiscriminately mingled, as chance had brought them together in the battle or the rout. Here and there amidst the slain there started up a gory figure whose wounds had begun to throb with the chill of dawn, and was cut down by his enemies ; some were discovered lying there alive, with thighs and tendons slashed, baring their necks and throats and bidding their conquerors drain the remnant of their blood. Others were found with their heads buried in holes dug in the ground. They had apparently made these pits for themselves, and heaping the dirt over their faces shut off their breath. But what most drew the attention of all beholders was a Numidian who was dragged out alive from under a dead Roman, but with mutilated nose and ears ; for the Roman, unable to hold a weapon in his hands, had expired in a frenzy of rage, while rending the other with his teeth.

No further proof is needed of Livy's realistic facing of the horrors of war.

Livy's own attitude towards war is Janus-faced. He saw its brutalities, its hideousness, but true to old Roman tradition he exalted the military glory of the Roman people.[158] He put in the mouth of the consul, Lucius Quinctius Cincinnatus, a sentence typical of Roman thought :[159]

"By some fate or other, we find the gods more propitious when we are at war than when we are at peace."

And at the end of his digression on Alexander the Great he descended to unrestrained boasting of Roman prowess in the past.[160]

Proud word I would not speak, but never — and may civil wars be silent ! — never have we been beaten by infantry, never in open battle, never on even, or at all events on favorable ground : cavalry and arrows, impassable defiles, regions that afford no road to convoys, may well occasion fear in heavy-armed troops. A thousand battle-arrays more formidable than those of Alexander and the Macedonians have the Romans beaten off — and shall do

[158] *Preface.*
[159] 3, 19.

[160] 9, 19, translated by B. O. Foster in *The Loeb Classical Library.*

— if only our present love of domestic peace endure and our concern to maintain concord.

Was not this long digression on Alexander introduced to point this moral at the end : an appeal for peace within the nation as a buckler with which to meet foreign foes ?

The classification of Livy's anecdotes and a re-telling of some of them seem to justify the historian's claim in his preface that the fruit of the study of history is the interpretation of life through noble examples and the consequent improvement of it. From his "pictured page" emerges a great pageant of scenes from religion, social life, politics, and war. An understanding of their themes is fundamental for a knowledge of Rome's life and history. Innumerable characters people this procession and become familiar as they appear and reappear. These descriptions of persons and of events is often colored by a deep emotion inspired by a noble patriotism. So these stories reflect both the ἦθος and the πάθος which Cicero demanded of his orator.

According to their subject and importance, the stories show great variety in length, for some are mere anecdotes, others are like those which the Italians of today call *novelle,* and a third class consists of long narratives which amount to inserted monographs. The technique of these groups varies with their length. In the anecdotes the qualities of style are brevity, clarity, vividness. The diction varies with the subject matter, ranging from the colloquial to the epic. Usually a single point is made and this is often clinched by a memorable phrase. In the short stories, also in the long narratives which cannot be analysed in this essay, rapidity, clarity, picturesqueness, realism or glamour, shape the author's art. Conversation is constantly used. Direct speeches are employed, often in pairs. The principle of contrast which appears in such balanced orations is used also in character study which often proceeds by comparisons of types and of individuals.

In all these anecdotes, short stories and long serials, the historian often speaks in his own person, commenting on style, on characters, on ethics and ideals, and giving sympathetic interpretations of great events. Partly through these personal interpretations, partly through the very telling, the function of the stories is seen. Their aim is moral instruction. Their ideals are shaped around the gods, the state, the home, the citizen, therefore they involve worship, patriotism, family virtues, civic virtues. Their humanity is eternal as these themes are eternal. And the stories give delight no less than instruction because of their unobtrusive, but consummate art.

Quintilian may summarize for us both Livy's conception of history and his success in writing it, for Quintilian appreciated the historian and the artist : [161]

History has a certain affinity to poetry and may be regarded as a kind of prose poem, while it is written for the purpose of narrative, not of proof, and designed from beginning to end not for immediate effect or the instant necessities of forensic strife, but to record events for the benefit of posterity and to win glory for its author.

In history, however, we hold our own with the Greeks. I should not hesitate to match Sallust against Thucydides, nor would Herodotus resent Titus Livius being placed on the same level as himself. For the latter has a wonderful charm and transparency in narrative, while his speeches are eloquent beyond description ; so admirably adapted is all that is said both to the circumstances and the speaker ; and as regards the emotions, especially the more pleasing of them, I may sum him up by saying that no historian has ever depicted them to greater perfection.

[161] Quintilian, *I. O. X.* 1, 31 and 101, translated by H. E. Butler in *The Loeb Classical Library.* Compare H. Taine, *Essai sur Tite Live,* Paris, 1904, especially chap. III. "Les narrations et les discours dans Tite Live."

IV

HORACE AS A RACONTEUR

As Cicero and Livy among Latin prose writers rank as peerless story-tellers, so Horace among the poets is the master of anecdotes. Those conversation pieces of his which we call Satires and Epistles from their very informal and colloquial nature demanded anecdotes as one of their methods of exposition, indeed as an essential factor in their style. French critics have appreciated to the full Horace's narrative art. I owe a large debt to Cartault's *Étude sur les satires d'Horace* and Lejay's edition of the *Satires*.

In this study I am not going to separate the Satires from the Epistles. They are written in the same metre, the hexameter, and so have the same art-form. Horace had one word for them, *sermones,* conversations. Though they were written at the beginning and end of the poet's literary career, their common informal character, their general themes, their self-expression make them differ only as informal conversations and letters of the same individual would differ. The Satires approach more nearly dialogues, are often in dialogue form. The Epistles, always addressed to one person, partake more of the nature of a diatribe and in the diatribe found their natural form since their subjects are constantly the doctrines of the philosophical schools. We may then consider them together as poetic *sermones* written in hexameter.

Cartault has outlined an admirable plan for a critique of Horace's use of anecdotes.[1]   It is necessary to consider their origin, their form, the part which they play in exposition : how they enliven it, so diverting the reader ; how they take the place of an argument or furnish proof of a theory.   A study of their distribution in the Satires will show that Book I is richly sprinkled with them but in Book II most of the Satires have the form of an anecdote.   The long third Satire of Book II contains more anecdotes than any other poem by Horace and should be studied in detail.   We must add to this plan the fact that the Epistles furnish many *exempla,* particularly of the philosophical type.

Horace's own comments on his writing of anecdotes and of Satires illuminate his use as Cicero's theories explained his practice.   In Cicero's style Thomas found sometimes too much of the orator, too much of the pupil of the rhetoricians.[2]   Horace, though he had received the same rhetorical education in Rome, is almost free from the savor of the schools.   And wishing apparently to incur no criticism of learning how to use *exempla* from them, he attributes his use of anecdotes to the teachings of his father.[3]

If I shall say anything rather frankly, or perchance wittily, you will grant me this privilege with a pardon.   My excellent father gave me this habit of noting certain sins for *exempla* that I might avoid them.

Small, true stories follow, told young Horace by his father as they walked together in Rome : of a spendthrift heir, of men ruined by harlot or adulteress. And through allusions to such scandals Horace's father showed him the more excellent way and shaped him as a lad to be true to the best traditions of Rome and to keep chaste, the first

[1] A. Cartault, *Étude sur les satires d'Horace,* Paris, 1899, pp. 165–73.

[2] Émile Thomas, *op. cit.,* p. 34.
[3] Horace, *Sat.* I. 4, 103–29.

of virtues. So Horace explains his habit, as an adult
writer, of meditating in promenade or on couch about
human frailties and designs for living. And through
this story of his father's moral teaching, Horace gives to
his own anecdotes an informal and genial tone that never
savors of the rhetorical schools where he was taught
their use.

Horace besides referring to the frankness and wit of his
anecdotes lays down laws for the writing of satire which
may well be applied not only to whole pieces, but to the
stories in them. It is not enough for a writer to arouse
the laughter of his hearer. Satire should have brevity
and rapidity. It should employ a style now grave, now
gay. It should play the role now of the *rhetor,* now of
the poet. Urbanity should give it restraint. Its key-
note should be laughter rather than acrimony.[4]

In another place [5] Horace through his comments on
Lucilius goes further in establishing the laws of his own
writing. Just as Lucilius confided his secrets to his books
as to faithful friends, so Horace uses anecdotes for autobiography. Indeed through the autobiographical element in Satires and Epistles, morals are often pointed by
criticism directed against himself. He affirms that his
stylus is used only as a defensive weapon to satirize when
he is attacked. But by delicate irony he often turns that
weapon on his defenceless self. Like Lucilius, Horace
has a moral standard in his *sermones,* for he is

> To virtue only and her friends a friend,
>
> scilicet uni aequus virtuti atque eius amicis.

All these comments by Horace on the nature and function
of satire are illustrated in his own writings in general and
especially in his use of anecdotes.

4 Hor. *Sat.* I. 10, 7-15.   5 Hor. *Sat.* II. 1, 28-70.

The sources of Horace's anecdotes are as diverse as the infinite variety of his interests.   Mythology furnishes him such familiar figures as Tantalus.[6]   Fables enrich his verses ; fables recalled by mere allusion (the sick lion in his cave, the viper and the file, man's two wallets, the fox in the lion's skin) ; fables related briefly, usually with dialogue (the horse that conquered the stag, the frog that imitated the bull, the fox stuck in the grain-bin) ; and one told at length, the famous story of the country mouse and the city mouse.[7]   Often he uses material from Greek literature even translating certain lines from favorite authors : Homer, Euripides, Plato, Philodemus, and Greek Comedy.[8] *Exempla* of both sayings and actions are drawn from different schools of philosophy : the dialogue between Aristippus and Diogenes, the anecdote of Polemon's conversion.[9]   History furnishes well-known stories of famous people : two of general Lucullus, one of lawyer Philippus, one of Villius and of Fausta, daughter of Sulla, one of the son of Aesopus and Metella, one of Eutrapelus.[10]

From contemporary life, he writes first of all autobiography,[11] but also in brief anecdote sets forth the scandals of the day.   The miser Ummidius so rich that he measured his coins, so sordid that he dressed no better than a slave, lived always in terror of dying from starvation.   But a freedwoman did him in with an axe, a brave new Clytemnestra.[12]   The singer, Tigellius, like all of his type would never perform when requested even by Caesar, would never stop when not urged.   He was inconsistent

[6] Hor. *Sat.* I. 1, 68–72.

[7] *Ep.* I. 1, 73–74, *Sat.* II. 1, 77–78, *Sat.* II. 3, 299 and 186, *Ep.* I. 10, 34–41, *Ep.* I. 19, 15–17 and *Sat.* II. 3, 314–20, *Ep.* I. 7, 29–36, *Sat.* I. 6, 77–117.

[8] Hor. *Ep.* I. 2, *Ep.* I. 7, 40–45, *Ep.* I. 16, 73–79, *Ep.* II. 3, 1–5, *Sat.* I. 2, 119–33, *Sat.* II. 7, 89–94.

[9] Hor. *Ep.* I. 17, 13–24, *Sat.* II. 3, 247–57.

[10] Hor. *Ep.* I. 6, 40–46 and II. 2, 24–40, *Ep.* I. 7, 46–98, *Sat.* I. 2, 64–71, *Sat.* II. 3, 239–42, *Ep.* I. 18, 31–36.

[11] Hor. *Sat.* I. 6, 45–64.

[12] Hor. *Sat.* I. 1, 92–100.

too in everything else, plunging from wealth to poverty, staying awake all night, snoring all day. There was no sense in him.[13] For consistency give me Volanerius, the gambler who, when arthritis crippled his hands, hired a fellow to toss the dice for him.[14] Avidienus, the cur, shows how thrift can run into sordidness, eating old olives, drinking sour wine and mixing his salad dressing with too little oil and too much vinegar.[15] These are a few samples of many references to the gossip of the day.

Other anecdotes are character sketches painted in miniature or on large canvases. Here is the tricky courtesan always weeping over pretended thefts of her money and her jewels until no one believes her tale of real losses.[16] Here is the too generous host urging on his reluctant guest a gift of pears which he finally admits the pigs will eat if his friend does not take them home.[17] The social climber appears as a bore on a walk down the Sacred Way [18] or at a Lucullan banquet for Maecenas.[19] The gourmand Catius lectures on gastronomy ; [20] the peasant philosopher Ofellus pronounces a homely diatribe on virtue.[21]

Anecdotal episodes form insets in Satires as in the case of the contest of two buffoons on the journey to Brundisium [22] or the sale of a slave in the Epistle to Florus.[23] Such episodes also make whole Satires like the lawsuit at Clazomenae [24] and the frightening of the witches.[25] All this list of subjects barely suggests the wealth on which Horace drew for his stories : mythology, fable, philosophy, history, contemporary life with its scandals, its types of character, its little events.

[13] Hor. *Sat.* I. 3, 1–19.
[14] Hor. *Sat.* II. 7, 15–20.
[15] Hor. *Sat.* II. 2, 53–62.
[16] Hor. *Ep.* I. 17, 52–57.
[17] Hor. *Ep.* I. 7, 14–21.
[18] Hor. *Sat.* I. 9.
[19] Hor. *Sat.* II. 8.

[20] Hor. *Sat.* II. 4.
[21] Hor. *Sat.* II. 2, 112–36.
[22] Hor. *Sat.* I. 5, 50–70.
[23] Hor. *Ep.* II. 2, 1–24.
[24] Hor. *Sat.* I. 7.
[25] Hor. *Sat.* I. 8.

More attention must be given to the varied form of the poet's *exempla*. Sometimes a familiar anecdote is merely alluded to. So in a Satire on the never-satisfied avaricious man a single verse sets him off in a myth : [26]

Thirsty Tantalus tries to capture the water fleeing from his lips. Why do you laugh ? It is about you the story is told with a change of name. You lie awake gaping at your money-bags heaped up everywhere and you force yourself to spare them as if they were sacred and to rejoice in them as if they were paintings. Don't you know the value of a coin ? What its use is ? It is its purchasing power.

Here the anecdote is interrupted by a query, pointed by declarations of fact and driven home by rhetorical questions.

Other anecdotes are told as insets in poems often in dialogue form. To present two opposite points of view toward wealth and patronage, Horace suddenly introduces a conversation between Aristippus, the Hedonist, and Diogenes, the Cynic.[27] It is clearly one of the *chriae* of the philosophical schools and so famous that it can be hurled in without mention of the names of the speakers at first. The point is made by praise of Aristippus' sense of *decorum*, the fitting, and by one damning adjective for the Cynic, the ill-adapted.

An anecdote in dialogue is introduced with like abruptness to conclude a Stoic Epistle on true virtue.[28] The speakers are identified at once, the good and wise man and Pentheus, ruler of Thebes. The conversation is a translation of lines 492–98 from Euripides' *Bacchae* ; but the climax made in it is a new one. When the stranger in the *Bacchae* says : "God himself whenever I wish, will set me free," he means : "I myself am a god and no mortal

---

[26] Hor. *Sat.* I. 1, 68–79.   [28] Hor. *Ep.* I. 16, 73–79.
[27] Hor. *Ep.* I. 17, 13–32, from Diogenes Laertius, II. 68.

tyrant can imprison me." Horace makes the remark refer to the Stoic conception of suicide, the ultimate path to
freedom which god has left open for the truly wise and
good man.

Another inset anecdote told in dialogue points Damasippus' accusation of Horace : that he is always trying
to imitate Maecenas though he is so much smaller and so
different from him.[29] Here the Aesopian fable of the
frog that imitated the bull is told with éclat and the lesson is driven neatly home to Horace :

> You are all swollen up over your poems !

A different type of inset anecdote is a short historical
narrative with incidental conversation. The story of the
soldier of Lucullus is used to explain why Horace writes
no more lyric poems.[30] There is a colloquial description
of this Roman O'Flaherty V.C. who, when robbed in his
sleep of his money-bags, performed a most daring exploit
in capturing an enemy's fort so that he might retrieve his
fortunes by his rewards. Later his general in a grandiloquent speech urged him to a second deed of daring :

"Go, my good fellow, go where your valor calls you,
go and a blessing on you. Magnificent shall be your rewards ! Why are you standing still ?"

The clever country boy replied, parodying the praetor's speech :

"The man who has lost his money belt, will go, will go
where you wish !"

From these tiny vignettes let us turn to longer incidental
stories written in narrative style. A good illustration is
the contest of the two buffoons in one of the stops on the
journey to Brundisium.[31] The style is narrative, the ob-

[29] Hor. *Sat.* II. 3, 312–21.   [31] Hor. *Sat.* I. 5, 50–70.
[30] Hor. *Ep.* II. 2, 24–40.

ject amusement.   The scene is localized, at the Villa of
Cocceius above the Caudine Forks.   The account begins
with an epic appeal to the Muse to relate the battle, a
mock-heroic, Homeric touch in contrast to the very colloquial diction of the rest.   The dialogue is a battle of
words with gestures.   Messius is called a Cock so that he
is one of the long line of chanticleers and as an Oscan is
probably taking the part of one of the stock characters in
the Atellan farces.   The jests turn on physical peculiari-
ties of scars and stature.   The whole object of the en-
counter is entertainment of Maecenas and his friends, and
Horace's telling of the episode loses none of its racy wit.

Very different is another story which illustrates the
wrong kind of patronage.[32] In a letter to Maecenas apolo-
gizing for not returning to Rome at his request Horace
does all honor to his great patron by showing how in spite
of all his benefactions Maecenas had left him free to live
his own life.   The picture of another patron, Lucius
Marcius Philippus, is presented as a contrast.   First the
distinguished old lawyer is identified.   Then follow
quickly shifting scenes in the story of his patronage of
Volteius Mena, scenes treated with cinematic rapidity.
Philippus going home from legal business in the forum
in the late afternoon saw a happy-looking man quietly
cleaning his nails near a barber shop.   Philippus' slave
sent to make inquiries about the fellow reported that his
name was Volteius Mena, his profession that of an auc-
tioneer, his property small, his reputation blameless, his
habits to make a little and to spend a little, his satisfac-
tions a few friends, a little home, the games.   Philippus
intrigued invited Volteius to dinner.   Volteius refused !

The next morning on his way to the Forum Philippus
came upon the fellow again busily selling his baubles to

[32] Hor. *Ep.* I. 7, 46–98.

the poor. He extended another urgent invitation which was finally accepted.

The third scene is the dinner-party where Volteius made every sort of break in conversation and didn't know when to go home. Philippus still kept fishing for his interest by dinner invitations and finally a drive to the country on the Latin holidays. That was a fatal trip, for on it Philippus, who had favored a back-to-the-land movement, persuaded Volteius to buy a farm and helped him finance the purchase.

The climax comes when Volteius after making a complete failure of farming finally one night all unkempt and wretched took his nag, rode to Philippus' house and begged him to restore him to his former life. "It is right," concludes Horace, "that every man should measure himself by his own foot-rule."

The most famous of all these long narrative anecdotes which are used as insets in other poems is the fable of the country mouse and the city mouse.[33] The imitations of it by Prior and Pope have made it as much a part of English literature as of Latin. Horace gave it a genial setting, for after dinner at the Sabine farm when his guests were discussing what makes man really happy, Cervius, a country neighbor, told his old wife's tale to illustrate the cares that wealth brings.

The story begins with the good, old-fashioned 'once upon a time.' The principle of contrast shapes the plan : country mouse, city mouse, country cave, city house, the Stoic frugality of the rustic, the Epicurean lavishness of the city gentleman. Friendship and hospitality bind the two old friends, but when the country mouse returns his friend's visit in a rich town mansion and is being entertained on the broken bits of a magnificent feast, suddenly

[33] Hor. *Sat.* II. 6.

in rush some Molossian hounds who drive them out in terror. The country mouse says good-bye with the moral : "This sort of life I have no need of, so farewell. My wood and cave free from attack will satisfy me with their simple fare." The humor of the story consists in the vivid descriptions of the costumes of the mice, their poses, their etiquette, their lively words. Horace's neighbor, Cervius, must have been an entertaining guest if he often told after-dinner stories like this.

In the second book of Satires all the poems except two and six are anecdotes. Six is autobiographical and contains the story of the country mouse and the city mouse ; two is in the form of a diatribe delivered by Ofellus, a dispossessed farmer, now working as a day-laborer on his old fields, but cheering his sons by his sturdy philosophy. Each of the others is an anecdote and is written as a complete dialogue. Horace's interlocutors are interesting characters, each selected as a type appropriate for the subject in hand. In Satire I, Horace consults the distinguished old lawyer Trebatius as to whether he should continue to write satire. Trebatius whom Cicero's letters [34] reveal to us as a temperamental, ambitious young officer in Julius Caesar's suite in Gaul, is here the famous old lawyer, literal-minded, exact, prudent, laconic, urging young Horace to use his talents to celebrate a new Caesar's exploits. Horace wins him over to approval of his genial, moral *sermones* by courtesy, puns, and laughter. In Satire III, a famous art-dealer of Rome who also figures in Cicero's letters [35] appears at the Sabine farm and lectures to Horace about the Stoic philosophy. This poem will be discussed fully later. In Satire IV, an un-

---

[34] Cic. *ad Fam.* VII. 6–22.

[35] Cic. *ad Att.* XII. 29 ; *ad Fam.* VII. 23.

identified Marcus Catius meeting Horace rehearses to him a discourse on gastronomy which he has just prepared. In Satire V, Horace does not appear but two Homeric characters, Odysseus and Teiresias, discuss the evils of will-hunting in Horace's own time. The conversation picks up a line in the Odyssey [36] and the humor, which is grim, consists in having the grand old seer Teiresias advise Odysseus to retrieve his shattered fortunes by the wily tricks of a Roman hunter of inheritances. In Satire VII, Davus, Horace's slave, at the time of the Saturnalia, uses his privilege of free speech and lectures Horace on his inconsistencies and his failure to achieve philosophic freedom. In Satire VIII, Fundanius, a contemporary writer of comedy, gives Horace a racy account of a dinner-party at which a *nouveau riche* bore entertained the great Maecenas. The narrative is full of comical episodes, witty remarks, and keen character portrayal.

One long Satire, the third of Book II, demands intensive study, for it contains Horace's richest and most varied use of anecdotes. In it, an antiquarian or art-dealer, Damasippus, making a visit at the Sabine farm, gives Horace a lecture on the Stoic philosophy. He himself when he had gone bankrupt had been saved from leaping off the Fabrician Bridge to his death by the Stoic Stertinius who taught him the philosophy of sanity. In Stoic style, Damasippus begins his diatribe with a definition : "The man whom wicked folly and ignorance of truth drives on in blindness is insane to the Stoic Porch." Cicero commends this methodology : [37]

Now every investigation which is undertaken on any matter ought to start from a definition so that the subject under discussion may be clearly understood.

---

[36] Homer, *Odyssey* XI. 139-40.   [37] Cicero, *de Off.* I. 7.

In another passage Cicero indicates the process of developing the theme which has been thus defined by examples : [38]

The method of discovering the truth is twofold for either we inquire what is the nature of the thing itself and how important — or we turn the speech from the subtlety of discussion to *exempla*.

Both these processes are used in Satire II, 3.   Stertinius is a popular preacher and employs all the devices of the sermon or diatribe : interrogation, the second person of the auditor whose character here varies according to the anecdote, picturesque descriptive words for realistic effects, concrete proper names, a varied diction of colloquial, poetic, technical, and Stoic words, and above all anecdotes.

The theme of Damasippus' diatribe is that all men are mad : the avaricious, the ambitious, the extravagant, the amorous, the superstitious.   This theme itself is the reason for the rich use of anecdotes.   Damasippus wishing to prove the insanity of mankind needs to cite the traits which reveal their madness.   The more illustrations he assembles, the stronger is the proof of his thesis.   So he gathers stories from all kinds of sources, from fables, the philosophical schools, Greek tragedy, Roman comedy, the contemporary stage, and in anecdotes he presents many types of character.

Oppidius forbade his sons to seek political office and try to win the applause which Agrippa carries off, for they would only be clever foxes imitating the noble lion. Damasippus declares that whoever calls him insane, will be called insane and will learn to look at the wallet of his own faults hanging unnoticed on his back.   He warns Horace, little man that he is, not to imitate great Maecenas, but remember the story of the frog that tried to

[38] Cic. *Tusc. Dis.* III. 56.

imitate the bull. The first two of these fables are merely alluded to in single lines ; the last is related in a neat little story with conversation between the mother frog and her son who had seen the terrifying bull.

Homer is a source for countless moral tales. Indeed Horace declares in Epistles I, 2, that the historian of the Trojan War teaches what is fair conduct, what is foul more clearly than the Stoic Chrysippus or than Crantor of the Academy. For the Iliad sets forth the high passions of great kings and the price that the people pay in war for their rulers' madness. And the Odyssey presents Ulysses to us as a useful example of what valor and wisdom can accomplish in the buffeting waves of adversity or against the Sirens' songs or Circe's cups.

The philosophers furnish two tiny moral tales. Wealth was nothing to the Greek Aristippus who in the midst of Libya ordered his slaves to throw away his gold since they advanced too slowly on account of the burden of it. The story of the conversion of Polemon shows how philosophy can save a sinner, for when Polemon after a drinking-bout burst into the lecture-room of Xenocrates, he was so startled by the discourse of the fasting professor that he tore the garlands off his head and then and there began to devote himself to the studies which made him the head of the Academy.

Themes from Greek tragedy illustrate madness. The avaricious man is just as crazy as frenzied Orestes when he killed his mother. Agamemnon accused Ajax of madness in slaying the sheep of the army thinking they were the generals, but Agamemnon was mad himself when he sacrificed his sweet daughter instead of a heifer at Aulis. Horace seems sane to himself but Agave did not seem insane to herself when she was carrying in her hands the head of her hapless son. The insanity of the amorous is illustrated by a dialogue between an excluded lover and a slave translated from Terence's *Eunuchus*.[39]   So both Greek tragedy and Roman comedy provide dramatic anecdotes for moral lessons.   The contemporary stage also is drawn on to prove that the mad are as deaf to warnings as the actor Fufius was once upon a time on the stage. Once when he was drunk he overslept his cue for the part of the heroine Ilione and did not wake up even when the whole audience took on the speech of her murdered son and shouted : "Mother, I call thee !"

Stories portraying different types of character are scattered lavishly from a full sack, not from a parsimonious hand.   One of the most vivid is of a miser.

Opimius who was poor in the midst of his hoards of silver and gold, Opimius who used to drink on holidays wine of Veii from a Campanian ladle and mere dregs of wine on working-days, once fell into a deep stupor so that his heir was already running around his locked-boxes and his keys, all full of joy and expectation. Opimius' doctor who was quick-witted and devoted brought him to by this device.   He had a table set up, his sacks of coins emptied on it and several persons set to counting them.   So he aroused his patient and he added also a word to him : 'If you don't guard your wealth, your greedy heir will carry it off at once.'   'While I am alive ?'   'Well, granted that you are alive, wake up.   Bestir yourself !'   'What do you wish ?'   'You are so weak : your veins will fail you unless a strong support of food be given to your falling stomach.   Do you hesitate ?   Come drink this rice-gruel.' 'How much did it cost ?'   'Only a little !'   'Just how much ?' 'Eight coins.'   'Whew !   What difference does it make whether I die from illness or wholesale robbery ?'

A companion piece is a portrait of an extravagant madman.   Nomentanus when he inherited a large sum, invited to his home all the sellers of fish, of fruit, of birds, of perfumes of Tuscan Street, all the cooks and parasites of the market and distributed his wealth among them because they were laborers and he was an idler who de-

[39] Ter. *Eunuchus*, 46–63.

served nothing. Today Nomentanus would seem a youthful communist rather than a madman, but Damasippus arraigned him for his folly. An even more spectacular case of extravagance was that of the son of Aesopus who took a beautiful pearl from Metella's ear and dissolved it in vinegar so he could drink it down.[40]

The folly of the superstitious is illustrated by the tale of a mother whose child had been sick in bed five months. She prayed to Jupiter for his recovery from his chills and fever, vowing that if he got up, on Jupiter's next feast-day the boy should stand naked in the Tiber. So if chance or a doctor gets the sick lad up, his crazy mother will kill him by placing him in the icy river. These are only a few of the anecdotal character sketches.

I have related enough of Horace's anecdotes in Satire II, 3 to show how many and varied they are. But the poem must be read as a whole to have these brilliant pieces fall into the pattern of his mosaic as essential parts of the design. Then the use of anecdotes seems the outpouring of a rich mind which presents ideas in concrete pictures of which it has an inexhaustible store.

Lejay in his summary of the structure of this poem points out that the discourse of Stertinius is a diatribe reported by a disciple. Horace has made this formal discourse serve the art of his exposition and by subtle irony has delicately satirized the philosophers by presenting their extravagant claims. He has arranged the discussion skillfully as an inset in a dialogue. He has given new life to the sayings of the philosophers by selecting anecdotes suited to Roman taste and by giving to a tedious lecture the piquancy of a scandalous society column in a newspaper. He has concealed the monotony of the invective by the variety of his style. He has kept the reader

[40] The same story is told of Cleopatra in Pliny *N. H.* IX. 58, 117.

at work by his clipped, elliptical phrases which demand
the interpretation of imagination.   In a poem which
might have savored of the schools' dogmas he has shown
himself original.   He has modified fanatic dogmatism by
the advice of good sense and the doctrine of the mean.
And by a supreme irony he has set the whole at the time
of the Saturnalia as he did the lecture of Davus.   He does
not believe in the conversion of Damasippus any more
than he did in that of the money-lender Alfius,[41] for at the
end Horace says to him :

"O Stoic, after your losses I pray that you may sell all your works
of art at higher prices than ever." [42]

These comments on the use of anecdotes in Horace's
sermones are meant to be sign-posts pointing the way to
different by-paths along which his narration strolls.   A
study of the origin, form, and function of Horace's anecdotes reveals his narrative art and the part it plays in his
sermones.   His Satires and Epistles are seen to be based
on an anecdotal style involving dialogue.   Through the
stories run the qualities which he considered essential for
these conversation pieces : brevity, rapidity, a style varied
from the grave to the gay, using the voice now of the
rhetor, now of the poet, now of the philosopher, words
that suit everyday conversation but are sometimes illu-
minated by poetic flashes, or set off by mock-heroics, and
a spirit that is moral, urbane, and humorous.   Intimacy
and laughter, geniality and friendliness are the genii who
preside over these instructive poems.

[41] Hor., *Epode* 2.   [42] Lejay, *op. cit.,* pp. 384–85.

V

THE ANECDOTES OF A FABULIST : PHAEDRUS

ANECDOTES appear first in Latin literature as an independent art form in a collection of fables. Valerius Maximus, to be sure, in the time of Tiberius published a collection of anecdotes for use in the rhetorical schools called *Facta et Dicta Memorabilia,* but the nine books of his compilation are a school-book or handy compendium for rhetoricians like a minister's hand-book of stories today. They are hardly literature. It was a freedman of Augustus Caesar named Phaedrus who really made the anecdote an art form.

Phaedrus,[1] apparently seeking some type of literature which had not yet been brought from Greece to Italy, as epic, choral ode, lyric, tragedy, comedy, pastoral, elegy had been, found in Aesop a model suitable to the urge of his thought. Fables to be sure had been used incidentally by Ennius and Horace,[2] but no writer had elevated them to an art form by publishing a book of them. Here then was a genre fit for pioneer work.

Only meagre facts about the life of Phaedrus are known and these virtually all come from his own poems. Even the nominative form of his name, Phaedrus, does not appear until Avianus used it probably in the fifth century

---

[1] Title: *Phaedri Augusti liberti fabularum Aesopiarum libri.*

[2] Ennius in *Aul. Gell.* II. 29 ; Horace *Sat.* I. 1, 32–38, I. 6, 92, II. 1, 77–78, II. 3, 314–19, II. 6, 77–117 ; *Ep.* I. 1, 73–75, I. 3, 18–20, I. 7, 29–34, I. 10, 34–41, I. 16, 45.

of our era.[3]　He was a Thracian born on the Pierian Mount almost in Apollo's school for the Muses, closer then to learned Greece than was Phrygian Aesop or Scythian Anacharsis.[4]　He must have been taken early to Italy, for he read Ennius in boyhood.[5]　His education was clearly the usual Graeco-Roman training, for he quotes Vergil, Euripides, and Simonides.[6]　He knew the hard lot of a slave.[7]　At some time he became a freedman of Augustus.[8]　He wrote apparently from first-hand knowledge anecdotes of Augustus and Tiberius.[9]　He dedicated Book III to Eutychus, probably the famous jockey of the Greens in Caligula's time.　Through some of his poems he antagonized Sejanus and hence suffered exile and other wrongs.[10]　He had jealous enemies.[11]　He felt the burden of old age and need.[12]　These familiar facts of his life are reviewed because remembrance of them is essential for the interpretation of Phaedrus' poems.

I am going to include in my study of Phaedrus the Appendix Perottina, thirty fables believed to have been collected by Perotti in the fifteenth century from a lost abridgement of Phaedrus.　Contrary to Ellis, I believe with the majority of critics, that these are authentic works.[13]

Fundamental for interpretation of Phaedrus' fables is his relation to Aesop.　The question about the exact amount of Phaedrus' debt to his great precursor can never be solved.　The difficulties have been well summarized by J. Wight Duff in a succinct paragraph : [14]

[3] *Epist. ad Theodosium.*
[4] III. *Prol.* 17–20, 52–55.
[5] III. *Epil.* 33–35.
[6] III. *Prol.* 27–28 ; IV. 7, 6–16 ; IV. 22 and 25.
[7] *App.* 15.
[8] Title.
[9] III. 10 ; II. 5.
[10] III. *Prol.* 38–43 ; II. 9.

[11] II. 9 ; III. *Prol.* 60–61 ; III. 9, 4 ; III. *Epil.* 29–31 ; IV. *Prol.* 15 ; IV. 21, 1.
[12] III. *Epil.* 10–19 ; V. 10.
[13] R. Ellis, *The Fables of Phaedrus,* Oxford, 1894, pp. 19–28.
[14] J. Wight Duff, *A Literary History of Rome in the Silver Age,* New York, 1927, pp. 136–37.

The well-springs lay far deeper in primeval Aryan tales than Phaedrus could have dreamed, and on the other hand the fables which he assumed to be by Aesop consisted largely of accretions subsequent to Aesop's time. The primitive beast-story, so widespread an element in folklore, becomes literary when it is shaped either to satiric or to moral purpose. Some such shaping of the beast-fable lies at the root of the renown of the Samian slave, the actual "Aisopos," who flourished in the middle of the sixth century B.C. From tradition and experience — that great repository of practical morality — the Greek observer drew his store. But in the history of literature "Aesop" became gradually a vague name ; for later tales were freely ascribed to him as a kind of father of fable, and such tales enjoyed wide popularity among Greek democracies both as a convenient cloak for social criticism and as a simple form of amusement. In this respect, then, there is an "Aesopic" just as there is a "Homeric" Question. The supposed Aesopic fables . . . were gathered about 300 B.C. by Demetrius of Phaleron, once tyrant at Athens, and afterwards *savant* at Alexandria, where he did much to establish the great library. This Greek prose collection it was — altered and interpolated by Alexandrine scholars — which formed the basis of Phaedrus's neat version in Latin iambics. The same collection, it may be inferred from the reappearance of several stories in Plutarch (or in writings attributed to him) , was a source common to Phaedrus and Plutarch (or the pseudo-Plutarch). Further, there is ground for holding that the modern "Aesop" contains actually more of Phaedrus than of Aisopos, thanks to the influence exerted by Phaedrus in medieval times, mainly if not entirely through the prose-forms to which his verses had been reduced.

Now though specific information about Phaedrus' imitation of Aesop cannot be obtained, Phaedrus' own poems furnish illuminating statements about his debt. He pictures Aesop in various roles. Now he is a slave to a cruel mistress,[15] now a shrewd commentator on life (*naris emunctae*) quoting the familiar proverb of the snapping of the bow which is always strung,[16] now hunting with his lantern in daylight for an honest man,[17] now pricking the bubbles of self-satisfaction of a vain writer [18] or a vic-

---

[15] *App.* 15.
[16] III. 14.
[17] III. 19.
[18] *App.* 7.

torious athlete.[19]   Then he doffs his tunic for a trage-
dian's trailing robes and mouths the tragic lines of Euripides stalking loftily on unfamiliar buskins to try to please
some carping Cato critic.[20]   More often he is made to
assume the character of the Cynic preacher, is dubbed
sophus [21] and *pater* [22] and gives out miniature diatribes
now on life's changing fortunes which bring *dolor et
gaudium*,[23] now on the success of the wicked,[24] now on a
growing boy's need of his father's constant companion-
ship.[25]   Due tribute is paid to the eternal fame won by
his genius.[26]   And the people of Attica are honored for
setting a statue of Aesop the slave on an enduring monument

> That all might know that open lies the road
> To glory, not for the high, but for the brave.

> patere honoris scirent ut cuncti viam
> nec generi tribui sed virtuti gloriam.[27]

Phaedrus states clearly and repeatedly that Aesop was
his model.   He has polished off in *senarii* the subject matter which Aesop found.[28]   Aesop was the pioneer in the
field of fable,[29] and Phaedrus uses his stylus.[30]   Aesop invented, Phaedrus' hand carried on the work.[31]

In some poems Phaedrus claims more for his own work,
and calls his fables 'Aesopian' rather than 'fables of Aesop'
giving as his reason that while Aesop wrote a few, he himself has written many using the old genre, but new subjects.[32]   Finally he admits that while he has always acknowledged his debt to Aesop, he has sometimes attached

[19] *App.* 11.
[20] IV. 7.
[21] *App.* 2 ; IV. 17.
[22] *App.* 18.
[23] IV. 17.
[24] II. 3.
[25] *App.* 10.

[26] III. *Prol.* 53.
[27] II. 9, 1–4.
[28] I. *Prol.*
[29] II. 9, 5–6.
[30] III. *Prol.* 29.
[31] IV. 21.
[32] IV. *Prol.* 10–13.

Aesop's name to his poems to give them the prestige of a distinguished writer and of antiquity.[33]   It is clear also though never stated by Phaedrus that he attributes to Aesop certain beast stories with evident political implications to conceal contemporary Roman references.[34]   In general, however, Phaedrus seems to have stated fully and fairly his relation to his precursor in the field of fable.

A Roman writer who certainly influenced Phaedrus though not mentioned by him is Horace.   Terzaghi in a chapter on *"Fedro Satirico"* gives a penetrating analysis of their relationship.[35]   Different as their forms are, Horace and Phaedrus have a real affinity because of their moral purpose in their satire.   In poems of each there appears a spirit of rebellion against the injustices of the times. Horace after his disastrous war experience at Philippi was driven by poverty to write verses,[36] and in his great sixteenth Epode revolted against the aftermath of the civil war with its lowered morality, its economic depression, its military prepotency so that he begged the brave to go into exile with him to found a new state in a new world.   A similar spirit of rebellion against tyranny, informers, and the oppression of the weak inspired Phaedrus to write many of his fables.

There are also general moral teachings, in part inherited from the practical ethics of the Cynic preachers, which are common to Horace and Phaedrus.   Avarice, the sin against which Horace inveighs most violently, is the theme of several of Phaedrus' fables.[37]   Closer verbal resemblances are seen in several instances. Horace's moral

naturam expellas furca tamen usque recurret [38]

[33] V. *Prol.*
[34] e.g. I. 2, I. 6.
[35] Nicola Terzaghi, "Per la Storia della Satira," Torino, 1932. See also Paul Lejay, *op. cit.,* pp. lxxix–lxxx.

[36] Hor. *Ep.* II. 2, 49 ff.
[37] Hor. *Sat.* I. 1; Phaedrus IV. 20, *App.* 1.
[38] Hor. *Ep.* I. 10, 24.

might be the title of Phaedrus' story of the conversation between Juno and Venus where the hen who is content with the smallest amount of grain provided she is allowed to go on scratching symbolizes women who cannot from the laws of nature practise chastity.[39]

Phaedrus' moral in the fable of the young bullock who tried to give advice to an old bull

> For the man who instructs his betters, this is writ,
>
> qui doctiorem emendat, sibi dici putet,[40]

is the motif of Horace's fourth Satire of Book I in which he replies to the critics of his writings and was used ironically by Horace in reply to critics of his morality in the third Satire of Book I.[41]   The thought of Phaedrus' *App.* 27,

> vulgus vult decipi,

is the point of Horace's anecdotes of the lover, Balbinus, blind to his lady's defects, and of doting fathers who overlook their boys' cross-eyes and bow legs.[42]   All these illustrations do not prove direct imitation of Horace on the part of Phaedrus but serve to show the affinities of their satire.

In two poems Phaedrus seems to have received definite inspiration from Horace.   In *App.* 6 the writer interrogates the Delphic Apollo and receives instructions from the god's Pythian priestess.   The poem opens with a prayer

> O Phoebus, tell us what is the better way
> Of life for mortal men.   Oh !   Hear my prayer !
>
> Utilius quid sit nobis, dic, Phoebe, obsecro,

39 Phaedrus *App.* 9.   41 Hor. *Sat.* I. 3, 19–28.
40 V. 9.   42 Hor. *Sat.* I. 3, 38–48.

which must have been suggested by the appeal made by Ulysses to Teiresias at the beginning of Horace's fifth Satire of Book II.   In each poem the prophet gives advice which is treated ironically : by Horace with fine subtlety, by Phaedrus in epigrammatic comment.   Horace puts into Teiresias' mouth words which are the very opposite of all his own beliefs.   Phaedrus attributes lofty sentiments to the priestess, but says that she goes mad because her words are so much wasted breath.

Again Phaedrus tells an anecdote of a soldier of Pompey which has such striking similarities with Horace's story of a soldier of Lucullus that Phaedrus must have used Horace as his model.[43]   Common elements in the two anecdotes are the contrast between the vulgar soldier and the magniloquent commander, the exploit of uncommon valor and the venality of the so-called hero.   Horace used his anecdote to explain why he does not write poems, now that the pinch of poverty does not constrain him.   It is introduced abruptly and his correspondent Florus is left to make the application. Similarly Phaedrus does not attach a moral to his tale.   Phaedrus, Terzaghi thinks, got from Horace the idea of interspersing among his beast fables anecdotes that are pure *novelle,* told for the story's sake, with only a vague ethical significance.[44]

This brief summary of Phaedrus' relations to his acknowledged model, the fabulist Aesop, and to his obvious source, the satirist Horace, prepares the way for a review of Phaedrus' self-criticism in Prologues, Epilogues and certain other autobiographical poems.   In his first lines he names his model Aesop and announces his metre, the iambic senarii.[45]   Further on he states explicitly that his

---

[43] Phaedrus, *App.* 8, Hor. *Ep.* II. 2, 26–40.

[44] Terzaghi, *op. cit.,* pp. 83–84.
[45] I. *Prol.* 1–2.

themes are not personalities, but life itself and human characteristics.

> My aim is not to censure any man
> But to show life itself and human traits.

> neque enim notare singulos mens est mihi,
> verum ipsam vitam et mores hominum ostendere.[46]

These subjects are to be set forth in imaginary fables wherein beasts and even trees talk [47] and in true stories, taken from contemporary life.[48]

Phaedrus claims three different functions for his poems : some are mere jests, written to amuse, to arouse laughter, with the aid of a playful Muse ; [49] others are to teach, to instruct life by wise counsel, to correct mistakes and make men more diligent in self-improvement and here jests are used to clarify a point or to illustrate a lesson ; [50] many poems that seem jests have a deep, hidden meaning for the wise ; [51] indeed fables were invented that oppressed slaves who did not dare to say what they wished might disguise their own feelings in beast stories and escape calumny by fairy-tales.[52]   Here the fable takes on a new dignity as the *vox populi*.[53]

> To jest I seem and with a frivolous pen,
> Since I have no great theme, lightly to play.
> But scan these ditties now more carefully.
> What benefit you will find in my weak verse !
> Not always are words what they seem to be.
> The look of things deceives, but the rare mind
> Can see what is hidden in some inner nook.

> Joculare tibi videmur : et sane levi,
> dum nil habemus maius, calamo ludimus.
> sed diligenter intuere has nenias ;
> quantam in pusillis utilitatem reperies !

[46] III. *Prol.* 49–50.
[47] I. *Prol.* 6–7 ; II. 9, 13.
[48] II. 5, 6.
[49] I. *Prol. App. Epil.*

[50] I. *Prol.* II. *Prol.*
[51] IV. 2 ; *App.* 5.
[52] III. *Prol.* 33–37.
[53] IV. 2, 1–7.

non semper ea sunt quae videntur : decipit
frons prima multos, rara mens intellegit
quod interiore condidit cura angulo.

Phaedrus gives too an adequate description of his style.
His usual brevity is a quality which finds critics. These,
however, he rarely gratifies by long narratives.[54] He claims
that while he uses an old genre, he introduces new subjects and in view of the great variety of themes before him
he has to remind himself that witticisms are pleasing only
when presented in moderate amounts.[55] Indeed he believes that each writer must have individuality, his own
thought and his peculiar style.[56] Yet he follows the
Ciceronian tradition about the use of anecdotes, as *lumina,* and as moral *exempla.*[57]

Finally as a self-conscious artist, he describes the audience for whom he writes. The fable of the pearl cast before the cock is written for those who cannot understand
him.[58] In the prologue-dedication of Book IV he tells
Particulo that he wishes him and others like him as his
readers, not the uneducated. For frowning critics whom
he dubs Catos, he dons tragic robes for a time but then
discards them when he finds that neither fables nor plays
(*fabellae* or *fabulae*) please the carpers who hurl vitupera-
tions even at heaven.[59] He will therefore write for the
intelligentsia, the *rara mens* which can discern even hidden meanings.[60]

This description of his desired audience gives special
poignancy to Phaedrus' account of the origin of fable.[61]

Now why the fable was invented first
I will teach briefly. It was some wronged slave

[54] III. 10 ; IV. 5 ; IV. *Epil.*
[55] IV. *Epil.*
[56] IV. *Prol.*
[57] Cic. *de Orat.* III. vii, 201 ; Phaedrus, II. *Prol.* IV. 3, *et al.*

[58] III. 12.
[59] IV. 7.
[60] IV. 2.
[61] III. *Prol.* 33–40.

> Not daring to express all that he wished
> Who wrote his feeling in a fable's form
> And by feigned jests avoided calumny.
> I broadened the road of Aesop's narrow path
> And meditated more than he had left,
> Choosing some themes to my calamity.

> Nunc, fabularum cur sit inventum genus,
> brevi docebo.   servitus obnoxia,
> quia quae volebat non audebat dicere,
> affectus proprios in fabellas transtulit,
> calumniamque fictis elusit iocis.
> ego illius pro semita feci viam,
> et cogitavi plura quam reliquerat,
> in calamitatem deligens quaedam meam.

In this and other passages Phaedrus lays emphasis on the fact that both Aesop and himself had been slaves ; that like Aesop he wished to speak through fables in behalf of slaves, the oppressed and the weak, and that he had done this even to his own hurt.   In view of these specific declarations there is undoubtedly political satire in many of the fables.   This is particularly clear in the first two books, which were probably published under Tiberius. Recurrent themes are tyrants, informers, arrogant freedmen, cruelly treated slaves, the greed of the powerful, the oppression of the weak.   And the treatment of these themes is so often tinged with pessimism, with irony, with sympathy that Phaedrus becomes the protector of the under-dog, the shepherd of the defenceless lambs.

It is natural to use in describing him metaphors from animal life because virtually all his political satires are couched in beast fables.   Two anecdotes which seem *per se* to be true stories are told without this camouflage, one of Augustus,[62] one of Tiberius.[63]   These will be discussed later.

The fable of the frogs who sought a king from Jupi-

---

[62] III. 10.   [63] II. 5.

ter [64] and received first a harmless log, then a water-snake who devoured them is said by Phaedrus to have been written by Aesop against the tyranny of Pisistratus. It is thus doubly covered, by attribution to Aesop and by fable form, from the dangers of contemporary satire of the Emperor Tiberius as King Water Snake. It seems possible however that Jupiter's message to the frogs

> "Because ye did not wish a monarch good
> Endure a bad one,"

is a satire of critics of both Augustus and Tiberius. Similarly the fable of the frogs' protest against the proposed marriage of the Sun is said by Phaedrus to have been written by Aesop about the marriage of a neighboring thief.[65] Editors generally believe Phaedrus meant it to refer to Sejanus' proposed marriage to Livilla, widow of the younger Drusus, so that there is real horror in the question of the Frogs whose lakes have all been dried up by the Sun :

> What then will happen if the Sun has sons ?
>
> quidnam futurum est si creavit liberos ?

The fable of the wolf and the watch-dog [66] has for its title:

> How sweet is freedom I will briefly show,
>
> Quam dulcis sit libertas breviter proloquar.

The thin, hungry wolf envies the well-fed watch-dog until he sees the mark of the chain on his neck and finds that the dog cannot go where he wishes. Then like Horace's country mouse he finds his own lot sweet because it insures his liberty. Havet [67] ingeniously argues that this

[64] I. 2.
[65] I. 6.
[66] III. 7.
[67] *Rev. des études anciennes*, 1921.

fable refers to "an actual dialogue in A.D. 16 between Arminius, the Cheruscan warrior and his Romanized brother Flavus." [68]   Whether this interpretation is correct or not, certainly the fable is a frank plea for freedom.

This same passionate defence of liberty motivates the fable of the horse and the boar.   In the fight with the boar over their common drinking-place, the horse sought the aid of man and so became his slave.[69]

The oppression of the innocent is the theme of the first fable in the first book, the story of the wolf who made one false excuse after another for killing the lamb.   False witness against the innocent is portrayed also in the story of the dog and wolf who slandered the blameless sheep.[70] This is perhaps one of several fables aimed at the informers under Tiberius.   The interpretation gains credence because of the open commendation of Augustus' severe judgment of a freedman who bore false witness.[71]

This poem of sixty lines begins with a stately maxim :

> To trust or not to trust is perilous,
>
> Periculosum est credere et non credere,

which is illustrated grandiloquently by allusions to Hippolytus who was too trustful and to Cassandra who was never believed.   Then Phaedrus says in order that his reader may not make light of old myths, he will tell a story of what happened in his own memory.

The story sounds like one of the *controversiae* recorded by the Elder Seneca or the pseudo-Quintilian.   A doting husband, father of a grown son, was secretly informed by his freedman that his son was bad and his wife had a lover.

---

[68] Quoted in J. Wight Duff, *op. cit.,* p. 147, n. 2.
[69] IV. 4, used by Horace (*Ep.* I. 10, 34–41) as the fable of the horse and the stag with the same point.
[70] I. 17.   [71] III. 10.

(The freedman wished to be named as the man's heir.) The husband believing the accusation against his wife pretended to go away on a journey, came home in the middle of the night and went to his wife's bed-room. In the dark he felt for head on pillow and touched one with short hair. Instantly in his mad jealousy he ran his sword through the intruder's breast only to find when the slaves brought lights, that he had killed his young son whom his mother had had sleep beside her to protect his chastity. At the sight of his innocent wife who was sleeping quietly, the father fell upon his own sword.

As the wife inherited the property, she came under suspicion and was taken to Rome for trial before the centumviri. After her lawyers had defended her valiantly, the judges, since the case was puzzling, appealed to Augustus for a decision. The emperor, after he had dispelled the clouds of calumny and found the sure spring of truth, gave judgment :

'Let the freedman pay the price of his great sin.
The woman who has lost husband and son
Is to be pitied more than to be condemned.
If only the father had but tested the charge,
If he had filed away all falsity,
He would not thus have cut down the whole tree
Of his home by a crime that severed root and branch.'

'Luat' inquit 'poenas causa libertus mali.
namque orbam nato simul et privatam viro
miserandam potius quam damnandam existimo.
quodsi delata perscrutatus crimina
paterfamilias esset, si mendacium
subtiliter limasset, a radicibus
non evertisset scelere funesto domum.'

Here the story should have ended but Phaedrus weakens his narrative by seven garrulous lines expanding the theme of not being too credulous and then apologizes for his loquacity by saying he has set forth his ideas in many

words because some have been offended by his brevity.
Now since Phaedrus usually shows a rather keen awareness of the art of narration, he may here again be camou-
flaging by wordiness his political satire about informers,
the real theme of this 'true story.'

Terzaghi sees not only in this anecdote,[72] but also in
the fable of the bearded she-goats,[73] satire on freedmen.
Certainly Jupiter's reply to the indignant rams : "Let the
nanny-goats keep their beards : they will never equal
your strength," may well have been aimed at the effem-
inate freedmen of Claudius' age.

Many of the beast fables portray powerful animals who
are greedy and oppress the weak.   The lion appropriates
the whole carcass of a stag and will not share it with cow,
goat and sheep.[74]   The simple-minded doves who make
a hawk their king are one by one devoured by him.[75] The
crow boring into the back of a helpless sheep declares he
knows whom he can injure and whom he must craftily
flatter.[76]   In the battle of the mice and the weasels the
leaders of the mice who have put horns on their heads as
standards for their ranks to follow in battle were so conspicuous that they were slaughtered, while their humble
followers escaped.[77]   In all these the protest against in-
justice is veiled in fable, but in two others the cruelty
shown slaves is described openly.

In one a hot-headed youth used to torture the family
slaves by flogging when his father's eyes were not on
him.[78]   In another a slave who is starting to run away
from a cruel master confides in Aesop his miseries : [79]

I am rich in blows ; I am very poor in food.
To the country sent, I get no coin for the trip.

---

[72] See Terzaghi, *op. cit.*, p. 85.
[73] IV. 16. Terzaghi, *op. cit.*, p. 66.
[74] I. 5.
[75] I. 31.

[76] *App.* 24.
[77] IV. 6.
[78] *App.* 10.
[79] *App.* 18.

If dinner's at home, I stand up all the night.
If master dines out, I lie on the road till dawn.
I earned my freedom, yet white-haired I'm a slave.
If I ever had sinned, I could patiently bear my wrongs.
Hungry I am and I serve a cruel lord.
For these and other reasons too long to tell
I've decided now to take to my heels and flee.

plagae supersunt, desunt mihi cibaria.
subinde ad villam mittor sine viatico.
domi si cenat, totis persto noctibus ;
sive est vocatus, iaceo in lucem in semita.
emerui libertatem, canus servio.
ullius essem culpae mihi si conscius,
aequo animo ferrem.   numquam sum factus satur,
et super infelix saevum patior dominium.
has propter causas et quas longum est promere
abire destinavi quo tulerint pedes.

The tragedy of this story is the pessimism with which Phaedrus makes Aesop advise the slave to return to his master for fear of what he would suffer if he ran away and were recaptured.

This facing of hard realities finds expression also in bitter generalizations :

> When change of rulers happens in a state,
> 'Tis but a change of name unto the poor.

> In principatu commutando civium
> nil praeter domini nomen mutant pauperes.[80]

> Once when a boy I read a certain truth :
> 'Plebeians pay for muttering openly,'

> ego, quondam legi quam puer sententiam,
> 'Palam muttire plebeio piaculum est.' [81]

Enough fables, anecdotes and morals have been cited to enable us to return to Phaedrus' autobiographical lines about Sejanus with some certainty of their meaning. Phaedrus' poems give evidence that he knew firsthand the hard

[80] I. 15.   [81] III. *Epil.*

lot of a slave and the precarious existence of a freedman.   His own personal experience included accusations
brought against him by Sejanus because of allusions in his
poetry which resulted in calamity for him.[82]   This calamity may have been his 'fatal exile' to which he refers.[83]
Certainly he lived afterwards in Rome surrounded by
envy and the suspicions of enemies.[84]   It is not important
that we cannot be certain of the particular fables whose
political significance caused Sejanus' accusations.   In the
very themes of his beast stories and his other anecdotes
there is enough suggestion of criticism of existing evils to
explain why Phaedrus' poetry did him harm.   We do not
need to assume that he deleted offensive verses or that
Book II has fewer lines than the other Books for this
reason.[85]

A plausible theory of Phaedrus' life on the basis of
meagre evidence seems to me this.   As a freedman of
Augustus he was contented with his lot and paid tribute
to Augustus' fairness towards his class in his anecdote of
how the emperor judged a venal and lying freedman informer.   In this period he knew Horace's work well and
was greatly influenced by it.   Perhaps Horace in sympathy with this freedman, who was what his own father
was, urged him to write fables. Under Tiberius he wrote,
largely in fables, a picture of slaves and freedmen who
tried to curry the emperor's favor and made a living by
informing.   Many poems are inspired by horror of tyrants and of *delatores,* by thoughts of cruel oppression of
the weak and loss of liberty.   His writings as he became
like Aesop the voice of the people so offended Sejanus that
he caused heavy calamity to Phaedrus, which was probably exile.   Perhaps a contributory cause to this fate was

[82] III. *Prol.* 38–44.
[83] II. 9.
[84] II. 9 ; III. *Prol. ;* III. 9, 4 ; III.

Epil. 29–31 ; IV. *Prol.* 15 ; IV. 21, 1.
[85] Terzaghi, *op. cit.,* p. 62.

his evident devotion to Augustus and to the Julian line
in the terrible conflict over the succession between the
Julian and Claudian branches of the emperor's family in
which Sejanus played such a scheming and self-seeking
part.[86]

After Sejanus' fall he was again in Rome, but uneasy
because of his enemies,[87] perhaps friends of Sejanus many
of whom kept working covertly against Tiberius.   He
knew a pressure of need that forced him to court the favor of a jockey of Caligula [88] and the aid of a Particulo.[89]
Finally the strength of the old hunting dog (for so he pictures himself) was broken, but not his spirit.[90]

Besides these anecdotes in which Phaedrus represents
the voice of the people there are others, rather a large
group, in which like the Cynic preacher he gives out wise
counsels about life.   Several picturesque ones deal with
women.   A short skit satirizes the devotion of a courtesan.[91]   Her lover has been too often deceived to believe
her protestation :

> 'Though many suitors bring me many gifts,
> In spite of all I love you most of all !'
> 'My light' he said 'I gladly hear your words.
> I doubt your faith, but find you very fair.'
>
> sic insidiatrix 'Plures muneribus licet
> contendant, ego te plurimi facio tamen.'
> 'Lubenter' inquit 'mea lux, hanc vocem audio,
> non quod fidelis, sed quod iucunda es mihi.'

A longer narrative about woman's frailty is the famous
story of the woman of Ephesus.[92]   The superscription is

A widow and a soldier :
how great are the faithlessness and lust of women.

[86] F. B. Marsh, *The Reign of Tiberius*, London, 1931, Chap. VII,
"The Struggle for the Succession."
[87] III. *Epil.*
[88] III. *Prol.*

[89] IV. *Prol.*
[90] V. 10.
[91] *App.* 27.
[92] *App.* 13.

The thirty lines of Phaedrus' poem relate rapidly the facts. A devoted wife who had lost her husband had immured herself in his tomb and, by her vow to live out her life there, had won fame as the most chaste of women. Near by was the place where thieves who had robbed the temple of Jupiter were crucified. Guards had been stationed there to prevent any one from removing the corpses. One guard becoming thirsty in the middle of the night, seeing a light in the tomb, went and asked the maid who attended her mistress for water. When the door was opened a little, the soldier saw a beautiful lady and fell in love at once. Every night on some excuse he came back until by his persistence and the maid's aid he won the woman. One night in his absence a body was stolen from a cross. In terror he told his mistress. She bade him cheer up and gave him her husband's corpse to nail on the cross that he might not pay the penalty of his negligence. The story is told with brutal realism but Phaedrus ends with a frigid moral :

> Thus baseness often steals the seat of fame,
>
> sic turpitudo laudis obsedit locum,

which destroys the ironic flavor of the narrative and turns it into a sermon.[93] The seriousness of the narrative is at the antipodes from Petronius' brilliant style and ironic laughter.[94]

The theme of the last two anecdotes, that all women are lustful, is asserted as a general truth by no less an authority than Venus. When Juno was praising the chastity of a wife content with one husband, Venus told her the fable of the hen who on being asked how much grain

[93] Terzaghi, *op. cit.*, p. 84.   [94] *Satyricon*, 111–13.

she would need to prevent her from scratching, replied
that a whole granary would not stop her from scratching.

> 'Tis said that Juno laughed at Venus' jests
> For well she knew the hen meant womankind.' [95]

A long and amusing story of the riddle of a will is told
in the style of the *controversiae* of the rhetorical schools.[96]
A certain man on dying left three daughters, one a beauty,
who hunted men with her eyes, a second a frugal country
girl fond of spinning, a third who was devoted to wine and
very homely. The old father made their mother his heir
on condition that she divide his fortune equally among
the three girls but with these terms :

> Unless they hold or enjoy their heritage,
> Let them lose the property that they receive
> And pay their mother each a hundred coin.

When neither the gossips of Athens, the mother or her
lawyers were able to solve the conundrum, Aesop read the
riddle by giving to each woman what was entirely un-
suited to her (city-house, jewelry, old wines to the country
spinner, fine raiment and attendants to the drinker, farm-
house, fields, flocks and shepherds to the beautiful flirt).
Each sold her inheritance, out of the profits paid her
mother a kind of inheritance tax and on the balance lived
her own life ! The wisdom of Aesop is made the moral
of the story. The interest of it is really in the character
drawing of the three daughters and the father's estimate
of them.

The story of Augustus' denunciation of the freedman
who gave false information against an innocent wife
thereby wrecking the happiness of a family has already
been told as an illustration of Augustus' attitude towards

[95] *App.* 9.   [96] IV. 5.

delatores.[97]   The story illustrates also Augustus' interest in supporting an honorable wife who through no fault of her own has lost husband and son.

Another favorite theme in Phaedrus' ethical sermons is avarice.   This is developed once in a poem which combines a fable and a diatribe.[98]   A fox when digging his lair came on an underground cave where a dragon guarded hidden treasure.   With polite apologies for intrusion the fox inquired what reward the dragon received for his sleepless vigils in the dark : did he take a part of the treasure for himself, or give a part to any man. The dragon had to answer no, but this was his fate.   The wise fox declared frankly that such a fate is the gift of wrathful gods.

Hereupon Phaedrus turns upon the avaricious man with his query :

> You who will pass where former men have gone,
> Why in your blindness rack your wretched soul ?
> To you I speak, O Miser, joy of your heir.
> You cheat the gods of their due, yourself of food.
> You are gloomy when you hear the lyre's strains.
> The jocund pipes awake no joy in you.
> You groan aloud over the price of food.
> You pinch and save to increase your heritage,
> And weary heaven by sordid perjuries.
> You cut down all the expense of your funeral
> Lest the Death Goddess find you a source of gain.

This character sketch of the miser is balanced by a story of the poet Simonides who despised riches.[99]   Simonides had become very wealthy in his travels through Asia from the pay he received for songs in honor of victors.   On his voyage home to Cios he was shipwrecked, and after remarking "All my possessions are with myself," saved nothing.   The others on the boat tried to save their money

97 III. 10. See pp. 106–108.   99 IV. 22.
98 IV. 20.

belts and their choice possessions, but some were drowned by the weight, others who swam ashore were robbed by pirates. Simonides who had carried nothing with him was received by a wealthy admirer at Clazomenae and presented with everything a man could need. It was rather priggish of the poet when his destitute ship-mates came around begging for food to remark :

> I told you all my goods were in myself,
> The wealth you carried off was easily lost.

The story however makes an easily remembered illustration for Phaedrus' theme :

> The learned man has always wealth within.

> homo doctus in se semper divitias habet.

Hercules furnishes another proof that riches are evil and are rightly despised by the brave.[100]

> When Hercules for his valor went to heaven
> He greeted all the Gods who welcomed him.
> But on the approach of Plutus looked away.
> To Jupiter who asked the cause he said :
> 'I hate the god of wealth who favors wrong
> And ruins men by bribes of evil gain.'

> Caelo receptus propter virtutem Hercules,
> cum gratulantes persalutasset deos,
> veniente Pluto, qui Fortunae est filius,
> avertit oculos.   causam quaesivit Pater.
> 'Odi' inquit 'illum quia malis amicus est,
> simulque obiecto cuncta corrumpit lucro.' [101]

In contrast to these ethical poems and many others like them with a moral attached are some that seem written primarily to amuse.   Such are the stories of Tiberius and the slave, the farmer and the pig and the conceited flute-

---

[100] IV. 12. [101] For other "veritables 'chries' " see Lejay, *op. cit.*, p. lxxx.

player. The anecdote of Tiberius [102] Phaedrus says is a
true story told to improve a race of busybodies at Rome
who are a great nuisance always strenuously doing nothing. Once when Tiberius had stopped on his way to
Naples at his villa at Misenum such a person, a slave in
the house, tried to secure the slap which gave freedom
by his officious attentiveness to the emperor. Wherever
Tiberius walked in the grounds, there was the slave running ahead of him tossing his curls, with his tunic bellowing out like a sail, sprinkling the dust of the path with
water from a wooden bowl. Caesar knowing the man
and his wish deigned to call the fellow and joke at him :

> This work is nought, your labor all in vain.
> My slaps are auctioned at a higher price.

> 'Non multum egisti et opera nequiquam perit ;
> multo maioris alapae mecum veneunt.'

Of course under the jest there is satire too, satire of the
ingratiating slave who would make the worst type of
freedman, but the little comedy in the park at Misenum
seems the real object of the true story.[103]

Entertainment is clearly the object of the story of the
buffoon and the country bumpkin.[104] A rich man who
was giving games offered a prize for the most original
novelty for his vaudeville. A well-known and popular
buffoon appeared on the stage of the theater without any
props and imitated a pig so perfectly that the audience
swore at first that he had a real pig hidden in his robe,
and then lauded him to the skies. A cool country fellow
said he would do the same stunt better the next day. So
the two appeared on the stage. First the buffoon grunted
and won loud applause. Then the rustic, pretending he

[102] II. 5.
[103] Some critics see in II. 5 "a too
distinct reflexion on the Sacred

Household," Robinson Ellis, *op. cit.*,
p. 5.
[104] V. 5.

had a little pig under his garment (and he really had one) pulled its ear and made it cry. The people shouted that the buffoon, their old favorite, had won. The country boy produced the pig from his garment and shouted back :

> Behold ! What sort of judges are ye all !

Of course this story of the vaudeville has for its theme the prejudices of mankind, but this moral of the first three lines is forgotten in the amusing tale.

So in the story of Prince, the Piper, with the moral

> Vain mind begets as vain self-confidence,

the ethics are successfully camouflaged by narrative.[105]   A popular flautist, named Prince, had broken his leg on the stage and been at home several months. The people thought their favorite was dead. A noble who was planning games persuaded him, when he was beginning to limp around with a cane, to appear on the stage as a surprise. The curtain went up. The gods spoke as usual. Then the chorus started a song which the flautist didn't recognize with the refrain

> God save our Prince.

The audience rose. The flautist thought the imperial strain was for him and threw kisses to the crowd. The knights caught on to his mistake and had the song repeated with the same result. Even the people saw the joke then and poor Prince all dressed up in white tunic, white shoes, white bandages, exulting in the honor that belonged to the divine house of the emperor was forcibly run off the stage by the mob.

In the telling of all these stories, both fables and *novelle,*

[105] V. 7.

both short epigrams and long anecdotes, poems that express the *vox populi,* poems that instruct or amuse, Phaedrus shows a definite style of his own in his art of narration. Brevity and conciseness combine to effect a simplicity which conceals its own high art. Conversation and direct quotation enliven narrative. The pungent point which appears often as "the sting in the tail" of Martial's epigrams is used often by Phaedrus too with telling effect. He made use of the eloquent homilies of the Cynic diatribes, of the rhetorical displays of the *controversiae* of the schools and of the autobiographical revelations of the traditional satires. Yet with all his knowledge of varied technique he maintained simplicity and rapidity as the main traits of his narrative art.

The main criticisms brought against him are that he tacks frigid morals on to his stories, and that his beast tales are often untrue to natural history.[106] But moral lessons are an inherent part of the fable form and fables which make beasts talk are naturally imaginative writing bound to use a free licence : they cannot be scientific.

His literary greatness consists in his pioneer work in introducing the fable as an art form in the Latin language and in making the little story, or anecdote, an independent art form in the history of satire, worthy of separate publication. But his work seems to me most significant because he gave a voice in literature to slaves and freedmen, the class to which he belonged. And in those early days of the Empire under Augustus and Tiberius he saw in the rising power of the freedman all the germs of civic evils which were to develop into monstrosities under Caligula, Claudius, and Nero. Petronius, the aristocrat and *elegantiae arbiter* in Nero's reign, was to depict with deep irony and complete pessimism Trimalchio and his

106 R. Ellis, *op. cit.,* pp. 23-24.

satellites, their vulgarity, venality, and corruption which dominated the society of the times.[107]   Phaedrus, a freedman himself, speaks to his class of the dangers of greed for wealth, of the subservience that murders liberty of spirit, of the malevolence that swears to another's hurt. The freedman of Augustus shows a certain noble dignity in these simple poems.

[107] See Enzo V. Marmorale, *Petronio*, Naples, 1936.

VI

MARTIAL AND THE ANECDOTAL EPIGRAM

THE poet Martial often called his verses *nugae,* but he assured a friend that these trifles were something : [1]

> He misses what is meant by epigram
> Who thinks it only frivolous flim-flam,

> Nescit, crede mihi, quid sint epigrammata, Flacce,
>   qui tantum lusus ista iocosque vocat.

The apparent inconsistencies of his statements are explained by his ample literary autobiography. In prose prefaces, in scores of epigrams about his writing, Martial gives a full length portrait of himself as artist. Since much of this is pertinent for a study of his anecdotal epigrams, it will be well first to see the poet as he saw himself. As an introduction, a paragraph on the known facts of his life will frame our picture.

Marcus Valerius Martialis was born in Bilbilis, Spain, on March first between A.D. 38 and 41. His parents, Fronto and Flaccilla, gave him a good education. In 64 he went to Rome to seek his fortune. There he found patrons who had come from Spain, Seneca and Lucan, but their aid was quickly cut off by their ruin in the Conspiracy of Piso one year later. We know nothing about Martial's next fifteen years in Rome. Then in 80 when

---

[1] IV. 49, translated by J. Wight Duff.

Titus opened the Flavian Amphitheater he published his first book of verses, *de Spectaculis.* Four years later he brought out two collections, now Books XIII and XIV of his works, the *Xenia,* verses to accompany Saturnalia presents, and the *Apophoreta,* verses to be carried home from parties. From 86 to 98 he produced a new book nearly every year. Then when he went back to Spain, his Muse languished and he published only one more book, XII, in 102. Two years later, homesick for Rome, he died in Spain. This is the short and simple annal of a man whose wealth lay in his seeing eye and his panorama of Rome.

Not even Horace was a more self-conscious artist than Martial. He names his literary forbears, justifies his selection of subjects, characterizes his style, limits his audiences. As for his models, he will not imitate the writers Accius and Pacuvius who vomited out harsh words, the old poets whose songs fell suddenly over high cliffs : his style will run along on a smooth path.[2] Yet he has his traditions. Among the Greeks, Callimachus and Brutianus

Graium quos epigramma conparavit,

were those whom he would resemble,[3] and the wanton frankness of his words is the language of the epigram, already established by Catullus, Marsus, Pedo and Gaetulicus.[4] And if he had had some one to love, he might have been numbered in his elegiacs with Catullus, Tibullus and Propertius or in hexameters with Vergil.[5]

The epigram then has its traditions of style and theme. Martial makes clear, however, along what individual lines

[2] XI. 90.
[3] IV. 23.
[4] I. *Pref.* See Schanz-Hosius, *Ge- schichte der römischen Literatur,* München, 1935 ; pp. 555-56 ; II. 77 ; V. 5 ; VII. 99.
[5] VIII. 73.

he has developed both. He will not use the grandilo-
quence with which the banquets of savage Tereus and
Thyestes, the flight of Icarus, the giant Polyphemus are
described nor such themes.[6]   No old myths with their
monstrosities for him, but life itself : [7]

> What profit empty myths in sorry lays ?
> Read this of which Life says "It is my own."
> No Centaurs here, Harpies, or Gorgon face
> You'll find : my pages smack of man alone.

> quid te vana iuvant miserae ludibria chartae ?
> hoc lege, quod possit dicere vita "Meum est."
> non hic Centauros, non Gorgonas Harpyiasque
> invenies : hominem pagina nostra sapit.

Even the local color of Martial's epigrams must not be
borrowed from the Greeks : let the man born amidst
Argive cities celebrate in song Thebes and Mycenae, but
let us, the sons of Celts and Spaniards, not be ashamed to
repeat in our verse the harsher names of our own land,
rustic though they be.[8]   Curios in verse imported from
Greece or the East are not for Martial.[9]   Life itself, he
repeats, is his theme. And though he often writes in
jest, he shows respect for all persons, even the lowest.[10]
And his jests are harmless : they are not dyed in ambition, envy or bitterness.[11]

> For in my writings 'tis my constant care
> To lash the vices, but the persons spare.

> hunc servare modum nostri novere libelli,
> parcere personis, dicere de vitiis.[12]

How completely Martial was committed to the themes
of everyday life and the plain style that suited them is

---

[6] IV. 49.
[7] X. 4, translated by J. Wight Duff.
cp. XI. 42.
[8] IV. 55.

[9] II. 86.
[10] I. *Pref.*
[11] VII. 12, III. 99, V. 15.
[12] X. 33, translated by Hay.

shown in his dialogue with his Muse.[13]   The poet protests that he has written enough : he is read everywhere
and will be read when rocky pavements and marble tombs
perish.   Why should his Muse still take delight in play ?
But Thalia knew her poet and asked for what he would
give up his sweet nonsense.

'Ingrate, wouldst leave thy quips to play the sage ?
   Ah, sluggish bard, what more dost thou desire,
   Wilt take the buskin for the sock, aspire
To thunder savage war in epic rage ?

So might some bawling pedant cite thee — one
   Whom generous youth and ripening maiden hate —
   On swelling themes let prigs and dullards prate
Whose toil the midnight lamp sees yet undone.

Season with native salt thy merry lay,
   Show Rome her very self in word and deed,
   And so the piping of thy slender reed
Shall sound when clarion blasts have died away.'

"Tune potes dulcis, ingrate, relinquere nugas?
   dic mihi, quid melius desidiosus ages ?
an iuvat ad tragicos soccum transferre coturnos
   aspera vel paribus bella tonare modis,
praelegat ut tumidus rauca te voce magister,
   oderit et grandis virgo bonusque puer ?
scribant ista graves nimium nimiumque severi,
   quos media miseros nocte lucerna videt.
at tu Romanos lepido sale tingue libellos :
   adgnoscat mores vita legatque suos.
angusta cantare licet videaris avena,
   dum tua multorum vincat avena tubas."

True to his merry Muse, Martial kept on writing his
innocent jests.   He continued too to dare defend that
wantonness which, as we have seen, he asserted was the
tradition of epigram.   This very frankness of speech is

[13] VIII. 3, translated by J. A. Pott and F. A. Wright, in *Broadway Translations : Martial*, New York, 1924.

native Roman.   Even Cato should recognize the licence
granted to the festive games of Flora.[14]   The emperor
Domitian is reminded that in such jesting the Fescennine
verses, used at his triumphs, indulge.   And the poet declares : [15]

> wanton my page is, but my life is chaste,
>
> lasciva est nobis pagina, vita proba.

The jests of epigrams are no worse than the humor of the
Mimes which all go to see.[16]   Epigrams use the freedom
of the Saturnalia (now for the cup and the kisses, as many
as Catullus had !).[17]   Some books may even rival the
verses inspired by Priapus.[18]   And who will dare criticize
my Latin lines, when Augustus wrote those wanton verses
which show he knew how to speak with Roman frankness.[19]

Moreover all my books are not ribald : some were written in such a tone that they will never cause a blush to
chaste matrons : [20] others which honor the emperor
Domitian have been cleansed by religious purification before approaching his temple and speak with modest reverence.[21]

Martial is honest : epigrams to be read he says must
contain the risqué, salt and gall : that is, wantonness, wit
and sharpness.[22]   Yet they must not savor of sour vinegar.   The delicate flavor, the sweet and the winning shall
have due honor on his page.[23]   So he claims to have left
a clear self-portrait in his song : [24]

> Certior in nostro carmine vultus erat.

[14] I. *Pref.*
[15] I. 4 ; XI. 15.
[16] III. 86.
[17] XI. 6 and 15.
[18] XI. 16.
[19] XI. 20.

[20] V. 2 ; XI. 15.
[21] *Pref.* and 1.
[22] VII. 25.
[23] X. 45.
[24] VII. 84.

and he would have this inscription carved beneath a bust
of himself : [25]

> Lo ! he am I whose light verse yields to none ;
> Reader, thy love, not awe, methinks I've won.
> Let greater men strike greater notes : I earn
> Enough if my small themes oft to thy hands return.

> ille ego sum nulli nugarum laude secundus,
>   quem non miraris sed puto, lector, amas.
> maiores maiora sonent : mihi parva locuto
>   sufficit in vestras saepe redire manus.

The very nature of his little themes demanded certain
qualities of style which Martial recognized and extolled.
Everyday life rejects bombast and the grand style of epic
and tragedy. A Gaurus may attack Martial because his
genius is pusillanimous and the songs which he makes
please from their brevity. Gaurus indeed writes of the
battles of Priam in hexameters in the grand style but does
that make him a grand man ? Martial fashions to be sure
little statuettes, but look out, grand Gaurus, the giants
you make are of clay.[26] So Martial uses a realism that is
often startling and much conversation that comes from
morning calls and dinner-parties, chance encounters on
the street, scenes in theaters, and at the games. For such
poems brevity is basic and book as well as epigram must
be short. Then less paper is consumed, the copyist fin-
ishes his work in one hour ; if read aloud, a small book
does not bore, a dinner-guest can read you while his drink
cools.[27] The result of such brevity is conciseness, *suc-
cincti libelli,* and no epigrams are long from which you
can take away nothing : [28]

> non sunt longa quibus nihil est quod demere possis.

[25] IX. *Pref.,* translated by Walter C. A. Ker, in *The Loeb Classical Library.*
[26] IX. 50.   [28] II. 77.
[27] II. 1.

Variety must break monotony even in such short poems and style must be varied. Indeed even mythology is at times used decoratively to honor an emperor though comparisons of his deeds to the labors of Hercules savors of the turgescence which the poet scorns.[29] But the poet has to think of his audience, his reader, be that the emperor Domitian, the plain Roman citizen, the provincial in far distant lands.

"Reader, you are my wealth!" Martial exclaims.[30] So for success he covets the ears of a liberal emperor or a wealthy patron. No strait-laced Catos for him, frowning brows or stern ears.[31] Better the Attic ears of learned Apollinaris,[32]

> nil exactius eruditiusque est,
> sed nec candidius benigniusque.

If he accept you, my book, you will never be used as wrapping paper for fish or scratch-paper for school-boys! Martial exults because he is read not only in Rome, but in Vienne, amidst Getic frosts, in remote Britain.[33] Yet away from Rome, even in his native Spain, he misses the audience of his fellow-citizens.[34]

> Whatever is popular in my small books my hearer inspired. That subtlety of judgment, that inspiration of the subject, the libraries, theatres, meeting-places, where pleasure is a student without knowing it — to sum up all, those things which fastidiously I deserted I regret, like one desolate.

> si quid est enim quod in libellis meis placeat, dictavit auditor : illam iudiciorum subtilitatem, illud materiarum ingenium, bibliothecas theatra convictus, in quibus studere se voluptates non sentiunt, ad summam omnium illa quae delicati reliquimus desideramus quasi destituti.

[29] XI. 17 ; IX. 65 and 101 ; see F. Plessis, *La Poésie Latine,* Paris, 1909, pp. 593–94.

[30] X. 2.

[31] IV. 82, XI. 2.

[32] IV. 86.

[33] VII. 88, XI. 3.

[34] XII. *Pref.,* translated by Walter C. A. Ker, in *The Loeb Classical Library.*

Martial's critique of himself can be illustrated point by point in the cross-section of his poems which we are about to examine, the anecdotal epigrams.   But his self-appreciation has been presented not to shape an outline of study, but to give better understanding of the man and his ideals of work through his literary autobiography. We must now ask : what sort of anecdotes did Martial select ?   Had he the gift of story-telling ?   Anecdotes of the arena fill his first book.   Afterwards he uses many little stories which are non-satirical, the majority colored by horror, as well as the satirical anecdotes which are witty or bitter or amusing according as *sal, fel,* or *risus* predominates.

His book *de Spectaculis,* published for the opening of the Colosseum in 80, gives a realistic picture of the popular shows in the arena.   Criminals were punished by being compelled to enact myths.   Pasiphaë was mated to a bull.   A woman rivalled Hercules in slaying a lion.   A Prometheus on his rock was devoured by a bird.   Laureolus hanging on a cross was mangled by a bear.   Mucius Scaevola burned his right hand in the fire.   Orpheus among wild beasts and birds was torn to pieces by a bear contrary to history.   In *naumachiae* Thetis' Nereids sported ; Leander swam to his sweet love.[35]

In the fights of animals rhinoceros charged bull, tigress attacked lion, elephant despatched bull.   And one maddened rhinoceros goaded by his trainers made a record by tossing a heavy bear, conquering a pair of steers, and driving a lion on the hunting-spears.   When men entered combats with beasts, a pregnant sow wounded by the steel gave birth to her young as she died.   A bull tossed one bestiarius imitating Hercules to the stars.   But another fighter named Carpophorus won fame by slaying

[35] 5, 6 and 6a, 7, 21, 26, 25 and 25a, and VIII. 30.

a boar, a bear, a lion, and a leopard, and at the end was
still strong as well as unconquered.[36]

Miraculous episodes are recorded : a hind escaped
from the pursuit of Molossian dogs and running to Caesar's feet like a suppliant was spared.[37]   A pious elephant,
that had but recently conquered a bull, of its own accord
knelt at Caesar's feet in obeisance, feeling the presence of
a god.[38]   We may laugh at the miracles, but the horror of
such melodramatic execution of animals and the slaughter
of helpless wild beasts to make a Roman holiday would
seem incredible if we did not recall the crowds that have
considered lynching in the south a spectacle and the thousands that find Spanish bull-fights a national entertainment.

The stories of the arena are by far the most brutally
realistic of Martial's repertoire, but in the group of his
non-satirical anecdotes horror and the macabre often command attention by their gruesomeness.   There are few
political anecdotes and these are laudatory.   A tree which
Julius Caesar planted in Spain is celebrated as dear to the
gods and destined to be immortal because not Pompey's
hands, but Caesar's set it out.[39]   Domitian is praised with
a heavy mythology which compares him with Hercules.[40]
How the gods protected Regulus is demonstrated by the
story of a sudden fall of a portico near Tibur just after
Regulus had driven under it with his span of horses.[41]
Such are Martial's few political anecdotes.

Three stories of Stoic suicide are told with a brevity
and simplicity which make them memorable.   Four lines
encompass Arria's death-compact with her husband and
her last touching words.[42]

[36] 9, 18, 19, 22, 12, 13, 14, 16a, 15.
[37] 30.
[38] 17.
[39] IX. 61.

[40] IX. 65 and 101.
[41] I. 12 and 82.
[42] I. 13, translated by Sedley.

When Arria to her Paetus gave the steel
  Which from her bleeding side did newly part,
"For my own wound," she said, "no pain I feel ;
  And yet thy wound will stab me to the heart."

Casta suo gladium cum traderet Arria Paeto,
  quem de visceribus strinxerat ipsa suis,
"Si qua fides, vulnus quod feci non dolet ;" inquit
  "sed tu quod facies, hoc mihi, Paete, dolet."

The suicide of another woman is told with an effect of pure horror untempered by beauty.[43]   When Cato's daughter, Porcia, learned that her husband, Brutus, was dead, she found that her family had hidden from her all swords fearing she would take her life.

She cried : "Know ye not that death cannot be withheld ?" and with the words drank burning embers down.

A contemporary Stoic story is of Festus who when disease was choking his throat and spreading its black mark over his face, took his life, not by poison or starving, but by a Roman death.[44]   These small poems on great themes have from their very simplicity an heroic ring.

Stories of sudden deaths are numerous.   They seem told for their novelty, one with a touch of satire, several from sincere feeling.   A lion usually gentle suddenly turned fierce and killed two slave-boys who were raking off the bloody sand of the arena : it should have learned to spare lads from the Roman she-wolf.[45]   Deaths of children are recorded with tenderness.   A little boy who put his hand in the mouth of the statue of a bear was stung by a viper hidden there and died.[46]   Under a dripping aqueduct an icicle fell on a boy's throat and killed him though the fragile sword melted in the wound.[47]   A tiny girl was consumed by sarcoma of her face and tender lips.[48]   The

[43] I. 42.
[44] I. 78.
[45] II. 75.

[46] III. 19.
[47] IV. 18.
[48] XI. 91.

death of the little slave-girl, Erotion, stirred Martial to three of his most beautiful poems.[49]   Very moving is the story of her arrival in the lower world : [50]

> Dear father and dear mother : Let me crave
> Your loving kindness there beyond the grave
> For my Erotion, the pretty maid
> Who bears these lines.   Don't let her be afraid !
> She's such a little lassie — only six —
> To toddle down that pathway to the Styx
> All by herself !   Black shadows haunt those steeps,
> And Cerberus the Dread who never sleeps.
> May she be comforted, and may she play
> About you merry as the livelong day.
> And in her childish prattle often tell
> Of that old master whom she loved so well.
> Oh earth, bear lightly on her !   'Tis her due ;
> The little girl so lightly bore on you.

> Hanc tibi, Fronto pater, genetrix Flaccilla, puellam
>   oscula commendo deliciasque meas,
> parvola ne nigras horrescat Erotion umbras
>   oraque Tartarei prodigiosa canis.
> inpletura fuit sextae modo frigora brumae,
>   vixisset totidem ni minus illa dies.
> inter tam veteres ludat lasciva patronos
>   et nomen blaeso garriat ore meum.
> mollia non rigidus caespes tegat ossa nec illi,
>   terra, gravis fueris : non fuit illa tibi.

Sympathy for the unfortunate poor appears in many poems.   A young swineherd fell out of the oak from which he was shaking acorns for his swine and was killed. All his poor father could do was to cut down the ill-omened tree and make of it his funeral pyre.[51]   When Martial's young secretary fell ill, his master freed him, hoping that the joy of liberty might save him.[52]

---

[49] V. 34 and 37 ; X. 61.
[50] V. 34, translated by Kirby Flower Smith in *Martial, the Epigrammatist*, Baltimore, 1920.

[51] XI. 41.
[52] I. 101, translated by Elphinston.

> He tasted his reward, his patron bless'd,
> And went a free man to eternal rest.

In contrast to the tenderness of such poems is the macabre ghoulishness which fills the picture of a midnight accident.[53] A Gaul going home late to his lodgings caught
his big toe, fell and sprained his ankle. The huge fellow had only one slave-boy so tiny that he could hardly
carry the smallest lantern. Fortune helped him. Four
branded slaves appeared carrying the corpse of one of
their fellows to the paupers' burying ground. The little
slave persuaded them to put the body down and lift his
master up so his great bulk was hoisted on the narrow bier
and borne off, indeed a "dead Gaul" as the gladiators say.
An amazing vignette of slave life this, fellow-slaves burying their own or laying aside that duty to help out a little
fellow who had to look after his injured master !

Accident and sudden death are the themes of many of
these non-satirical epigrams. We may close our illustrations with a poem on the death of a city. Martial's
verses express the emotion which the traveler still feels
as he walks through the ruins of Pompeii.[54]

> Vesuvius, cover'd with the fruitful vine,
> Here flourish'd once, and ran with floods of wine :
> Here Bacchus oft to the cool shades retired,
> And his own native Nysa less admired :
> Oft to the mountain's airy tops advanced,
> The frisking Satyrs on the summits danced :
> Alcides here, here Venus, graced the shore,
> Nor loved her favourite Lacedaemon more.
> Now piles of ashes, spreading all around
> In undistinguish'd heaps, deform the ground :
> The gods themselves the ruin'd seats bemoan,
> And blame the mischiefs that themselves have done.

> Hic est pampineis viridis modo Vesbius umbris ;
> presserat hic madidos nobilis uva lacus ;

haec iuga, quam Nysae colles plus Bacchus amavit ;
   hoc nuper Satyri monte dedere choros ;
haec Veneris sedes Lacedaemone gratior illi ;
   hic locus Herculeo nomine clarus erat.
cuncta iacent flammis et tristi mersa favilla :
   nec superi vellent hoc licuisse sibi.

In a group of anecdotes that may be called satirical, there is little virulence.   In fact only one poem is really steeped in the bitterness of gall and Martial after writing it had to justify to a friend the fact that it was written in hexameters and at unusual length.[55]   The episode which called forth these thirty lines of invective was the fact that an unnamed poet had dared to emend some of Martial's verses.   A literary insult was never more fully avenged by abuse, derision, and warning.   Martial's assailant is finally advised to beware the bear that walks like a man and not to tempt an angry beast that is alive.

The one political anecdote among these satires contains more laudation than condemnation, for it is on the lot of political exiles and honors friends who share their fate.[56]

      See your great friend Caesonius, who is gone !
      His likeness seems to animate the stone !
      Whom Nero censured, spite of tyrant's hate,
      You dared acquit, and dared to share his fate.
      You, who refused a consul to attend,
      Attend through dangerous seas an exiled friend.
      If any names shall in my writings live,
      Or if my own my ashes shall survive,
      Let it in every future age be said,
      His love to Seneca, that you repaid.

      Maximus ille tuus, Ovidi, Caesonius hic est,
        cuius adhuc vultum vivida cera tenet.
      hunc Nero damnavit ; sed tu damnare Neronem
        ausus es et profugi, non tua, fata sequi :
      aequora per Scyllae magnus comes exulis isti,

[55] VI. 64 and 65.   [56] VII. 44, translated by Hay.

> qui modo nolueras consulis ire comes.
> si victura meis mandantur nomina chartis
>   et fas est cineri me superesse meo,
> audiet hoc praesens venturaque turba fuisse
>   illi te, Senecae quod fuit ille suo.

Satires on women are incisive and penetrating though brief. One curl on Lalage's head slipped out of place because a hairpin was not securely set by her maid. Lalage struck the girl with her mirror and killed her. Fit punishment for Lalage would be to have her head denuded of her hair, her beauty lost.[57] Proculeia has suddenly divorced her aged husband. I know why. He was praetor. The festivals he had to celebrate would have cost her thousands. This is not a divorce : it is thrift, Proculeia.[58]

Such poems as these might make us think of the bachelor Martial as a misogynist if they were not balanced by the tributes to the Stoic matrons and by certain exquisite lyrics to high Roman ladies. Delicately drawn is one cameo portrait, yet it contains a political appeal. A dove fluttered down to Aratulla's bosom as she sat quietly alone. It stayed there uncompelled. If it is right to hope a happier future for a devoted sister and prayers may touch the Monarch of the World, I think the bird came from Sardinia as a messenger of an exile to tell her that her brother will surely come home.[59] Another lady, Nigrina, lost her husband, Rusticus, in the far east (Cappadocia). She brought back his bones in her arms, complaining only that the journey was too short. When she gave the sacred urn to the tomb which she envied, she seemed to lose her husband a second time.[60] These poems in praise of women counterbalance the satires of a Proculeia and a Lalage.

[57] II. 66.
[58] X. 41.
[59] VIII. 32.
[60] IX. 30.

Very different from these last sober elegiacs are certain
merry satires on everyday life. A friend is reproached for
passing on to Martial all his own Saturnalia presents.[61]
At the end of a long list varying from seven toothpicks to
dried prunes, Martial calculates that the whole lot was
worth hardly thirty sesterces, yet eight huge Syrian slaves
brought them and he assures his friend, Umber, that it
would have been much more convenient for both of them
if five pounds of silver had been sent by a single slave-
boy. Another story tells how Mamurra went shopping
in Rome : [62] he looked over fair slave-boys, had elegant
tables and tortoise-shell couches uncovered ; he sniffed at
the antiquity of Corinthian bronzes, criticized Polyclitus'
statues, said crystal vases had flaws in them, handled old
goblets, even those chased by Mentor, counted the emer-
alds and pearls in earrings, hunted a real sardonyx, bar-
gained for large jaspers !

And when he left, worn out, as noon approached,
He bought two cups for a cent and carried them home !

Another picture of Vacerra moving in the city has more
sting.[63] You had to move, Vacerra : two years' rent were
due. Your creditors didn't leave you much to carry. Indeed your three women carried all : your wife with her
seven red curls, your white-haired mother, your portly
aunt. They looked like furies. And you were a pale
beggar. Such furniture, such remnants of noisome food,
even ropes stripped of garlic, and onions ! Why seek a
house and debts again, Vacerra ? With this stuff you can
get free lodging under the Bridge !

In contrast to the last is the picture of Bassus riding in
a traveling carriage near the Porta Capena where the

[61] VII. 53.
[62] IX. 59.
[63] XII. 32.

plain of the battle of the Horatii was green and the little
shrine of Hercules was thronged. He bore all the rich
supplies of the country : cabbages, lettuce, beets, birds, a
hare, a sucking-pig, and a slave even carried eggs in a bas-
ket of straw. Where was Bassus going, to the city ? By
no means : he was on his way to the country ! The point
is condensed into the one stinging line at the end. Could
there be better satire of a rich man posing as a country
farmer ?

Amusements at Rome have their share in satire. Philo-
stratus who had been out to a party at the baths of Sinuessa,
on coming home late, fell down some long steps and perished. He ought to have drunk water.[64] In the theater
Domitian's edict about special seats for the knights was
always causing trouble to would-be knights : the ushers
were kept busy getting rid of upstarts. Nixon has well
translated a pair of these.[65]

At the Theatre

The command of our master and lord
That the law must no more be ignored
 Which reserved fourteen rows
 As knights' seats at the shows
Seemed to most Romans rather untoward.
But to Phasis the law seemed a treat,
And choosing with care a knight's seat,
 Helped by grand purple vest
 And an inflated chest,
He remarked with aplomb most complete :
"Well, at last we can sit at our ease ;
I'm glad that we knights and the lees
 Of Rome's great unwashed
 Need no longer be squashed
All together and gratify fleas."
Stretching out he went on in this style
Till the usher caught sight of his smile,

[64] XI. 82.
[65] V. 8 and 14 ; Paul Nixon, *A Roman Wit*, Boston, 1911.

And nowise impressed
By the grand purple vest,
Gave it vigorous aid up the aisle.

Edictum domini deique nostri,
quo subsellia certiora fiunt
et puros eques ordines recepit,
dum laudat modo Phasis in theatro,
Phasis purpureis ruber lacernis,
et iactat tumido superbus ore :
"Tandem commodius licet sedere,
nunc est reddita dignitas equestris ;
turba non premimur, nec inquinamur"
haec et talia dum refert supinus,
illas purpureas et adrogantes
iussit surgere Leitus lacernas.

At the Theatre

Accustomed to sit in the very front row
   When the first comers sat where they pleased,
      Nanneius quite scoffed
      At new laws and as oft
   On the seat of a knight straightway seized.

But he found himself forced to keep changing his camps
   Since the usher was deaf to his prayers :
      When no seat was in sight
      He stayed nearly a knight,
   For he squeezed between two of their chairs.

With only one eye leering over his cloak
   That he'd pulled on his head in his guile,
      He took in the show
      Feeling quite *du monde beau*
   Till the usher next showed him the aisle.

At last twixt the seats of the knights and the plebs
   He crouched on one knee best he could,
      Telling those who were near
      He was sitting down here,
   But telling the usher he stood.

Sedere primo solitus in gradu semper
tunc, cum liceret occupare, Nanneius
bis excitatus terque transtulit castra,
et inter ipsas paene tertius sellas
post Gaiumque Luciumque consedit.
illinc cucullo prospicit caput tectus
oculoque ludos spectat indecens uno.
et hinc miser deiectus in viam transit,
subsellioque semifultus extremo
et male receptus altero genu iactat
equiti sedere Leitoque se stare.

Martial like Phaedrus directs his satire not only against the foibles and whimsies of mankind, but against men's callousness and cruelty. Poverty-stricken Gaurus in the name of a friendship of many years asked the praetor for a hundred sesterces, the amount he lacked for the money qualification of a knight. The praetor begged off because he was going to give a much larger sum to two jockeys. Martial's wingèd arrow aims straight at his heartlessness : [66]

> The shame, O praetor, of ingratitude !
> The shame, O praetor, of your evil wealth !
> Your gifts enrich no horseman, but a horse.

> a pudet ingratae, pudet a male divitis arcae :
>   quod non vis equiti, vis dare, praetor, equo ?

The last line with its antitheses and its play on words at the end of the two halves of the pentameter is not merely rhetoric ; it is a whiplash.

A picture of cruelty to a slave is rounded out in six lines with the same sort of effective sting at the end.[67]

> Thy servant thou for a great sum didst sell,
> That but once, Callidore, thou might'st fare well.
> Nor far'd'st thou well : a mullet of four pound
> Was the head dish, which the whole table crown'd.

[66] IV. 67.
[67] X. 31, an anonymous translation of 1695.

May we not, wretch, exclaim 'gainst this thy treat ?
Say, 'twas a man, not fish, that thou didst eat.

addixti servum nummis here mille ducentis,
    ut bene cenares, Calliodore, semel.
nec bene cenasti : mullus tibi quattuor emptus
    librarum cenae pompa caputque fuit.
exclamare libet : "Non est hic, improbe, non est
    piscis : homo est ; hominem, Calliodore, comes."

Martial has shown that the anecdotal epigram however tiny may be a satire no less than an encomium, a dirge, a laugh, or a jest.

This reading of the anecdotal epigrams, this selected group of Martial's poems, reveals fully Martial the poet and Martial at his best.   In the group appear some of Martial's most famous verses : on Arria, on Erotion, on Pompeii.   Revolting obscenity does not dim the lustre of this anthology.   The subjects illustrate his own statements about his writing, for he does not celebrate Greek cities but his native Bilbilis, Pompeii, Rome.   He does not tell myths but he writes about life itself.   His portraits of people are alive.   His anecdotes are events that might fill the pages of a city newspaper today : an emperor's safe return from war, a politician's escape from death, suicides, fatal accidents, horrible catastrophes to children ; sports (gladiators taking the place of pugilists, animals in the arena like Ringling's circus) ; scenes at the theater ; extravagance over racing, executions viewed as shows.   Martial too has his personal columns with news of divorces, of extravagant dinners.   We are looking at a technicolored rapidly moving cinema of Roman everyday life and the people in the scenes both move and talk.

The art by which Martial sets his stage is so perfect that it is forgotten.   His themes are not trite yet he was aware of both a Greek tradition and a Latin tradition for epigram and is indebted to the Greek Anthology and to Catullus.[68]   In his language he dares to employ words from the street and lyric diction.   Simple as he seems to be, he often attains the effect of simplicity by very rhetorical devices of balanced phrases, antithesis, play on words, climax that turns on the unexpected.   The richness of his vocabulary, the easy adaptation of different metres to different themes effect a variety of style even though always unity of theme is preserved.

Such masterly technique creates his characteristic qualities, brevity, conciseness, variety which runs through the gamut of sweetness and laughter, wit and gall.   Wingèd words in direct speech or little conversations drive points home.   Frank acceptance of life and power to operate a candid camera produce an unparalleled realism in miniatures and by his truthful, genial or satirical pictures of human beings in his stories he presents a composite photograph of his own personality in all its sincerity, its faults, its enjoyments and its humanity.

[68] James Hutton, *The Greek Anthology in Italy to the Year 1800,* Cornell University, 1935, pp. 21–22 ; J. Wight Duff, *op. cit.,* p. 524.

VII

THE ANECDOTES OF A STOIC :
YOUNG PERSIUS

In the reign of Nero a youthful satirist appeared who became the poetic voice of Stoicism as Lucretius in the age
of Cicero had been the voice of Epicureanism.   Aulus
Persius Flaccus died at thirty-eight so that his youthful
precocity never developed into the full artistry which
might have placed him among poets of the first rank.   His
claim to distinction therefore remains the fact that he was
the voice of one crying in the wilderness of dark days :
"Prepare ye the way of virtue."   So few persons, even stu-
dents of Latin, read Persius now because of the obscurity
in part of his poetry that it is necessary to introduce him
by a brief biography and an account of his relation to his
times.

   There is an unusually good *Vita* of the poet based on the
commentary of Valerius Probus.   He was born in Volaterrae in 34.   His mother was evidently of Etruscan stock
from her name, Sisennia.   His father who was a knight
died when Persius was six years old.   His mother remar-
ried but soon lost her second husband.   So a household
of women, mother, aunt, sister, was largely responsible for
Persius' education.   At twelve he went to Rome and there
studied literature under the eminent grammarian, Pa-
laemon, and rhetoric under Verginius Flavus who was
later banished by Nero because his eloquence was too fa-

mous.   At sixteen he became the pupil and friend of a
great Stoic teacher, Cornutus, who had an abiding influence on his life.   He was intimate with the distinguished
Stoic senator, Thrasea, through ties of kinship with his
wife, Arria, indeed he traveled with him.   Through Cornutus he met other philosophers, the Greek doctor, Claudius Agathemerus, and Petronius Aristocrates.   Lucan he
knew as a fellow pupil of Cornutus.   And the lyric poet,
Caesius Bassus, was a life-long friend.   Lucan's uncle,
Seneca, he knew but he was not attracted by his talents.
He died in 62 from some disease of the stomach at his villa
on the Appian Way eight miles from Rome.   His wealth
he bequeathed largely to his mother and sister, but left
his library including seven hundred books by the Stoic,
Chrysippus, some silver dishes, and a legacy of money to
Cornutus.   Cornutus accepted only the books.   To him
was entrusted the decision about the publication of Persius' works, and on his advice his earliest works were destroyed : a *praetexta* or play based on Roman history, the
Hodoeporicon, probably a book about his travels with
Thrasea, and a poem on the elder Arria.   His six Satires
were then published by his friend, Caesius Bassus.

Certain points emerge clearly from the *Vita.*   Persius
in social position was at the antipodes from Phaedrus, the
freedman of Augustus' household, and from Martial.
Persius was a patrician.   He was also wealthy.   His
friends were literary men and philosophers.   His life was
spent under the influence of a great Stoic politician and
a great Stoic teacher.   But in spite of the clarity of this
narrative, certain puzzling problems have evolved from it.
Was Persius a bookish recluse who knew nothing of the
society of which he wrote, or was he in touch with the life
of his age ?   Did he boldly satirize the emperor Nero under a thin disguise, or did he preach the religion of Stoi-

cism in general terms ?   A minor puzzle too arises in regard to what changes Cornutus made in the last book.   For
the *Life* says :

> Hunc ipsum librum imperfectum reliquit. Versus aliqui
> dempti sunt ultimo libro, et quasi finiturus esset leviter correxit
> Cornutus.

> This book itself he left unfinished. Certain verses were re-
> moved from the last book and Cornutus made some minor altera-
> tions as if he had the intention of completing it.

This essay is not the place for the textual criticism involved in a discussion of whether Cornutus deleted a fragment of a seventh, unfinished Satire, or part of the sixth
Satire to give it its present form.[1]   In regard to Persius'
relation to his times, I believe that a careful reader with
sympathy for youth in revolt cannot believe Pretor's accusation that he wrote "from an almost absolute seclusion
against the vices of a society of which he knew nothing,
and with which he had renounced all intercourse." [2]   A
young man who was intimate in the family of those Stoics
who were living purely but dangerously in a corrupt age
and were to die for their cause, a young man who had written a poem on the heroine, Arria, who shared her husband's martyrdom with a *non dolet* on her lips, was hardly
out of touch with life.   It was no "cloistered bookishness"
which produced such passion for noble living, such ardor
in friendship for his greatest teacher.   And many of Persius' descriptions savor of life itself as do Martial's epigrams, pervaded as they are by a realism based on observation.   A study of Persius' anecdotes will itself, I think,
refute this charge.

The third problem, whether Persius' poems contain a
veiled satire on the emperor Nero, depends for solution

---

[1] For a summary of theories, see A. Pretor, *A. Persii Flacci Satirarum Liber,*
London, 1868, pp. xix–xxii.

[2] *Ibid.,* p. xiii.

so largely on subjective interpretation that no conclusive decision can be reached about it.   Personally I am convinced that in the first poem there is general satire of third-rate poetasters rather than particular satire of Nero's poetic effusions, and I prefer to follow the manuscript reading of the key-note sentence

> Auriculas asini quis non habet ?
>
> Who has not the ears of an ass ?

rather than the tradition in the *Vita* that *Midas rex* stood here originally and represented Nero.[3]   And I cannot see in the anecdotal character sketch of Alcibiades in the fourth Satire a yet more direct attack on Nero.[4]   Obvious satirical references to the emperor would hardly have been published by Cornutus and Caesius Bassus at a time when such *lèse majesté* might have imperiled Persius' living friends.

Rather I find in Persius' poems, not personal satire of individuals, but a passion to make known in degenerate times the true meaning of life as he had learned it from his great Stoic teacher : that the most valuable possession of man is liberty of spirit ; that virtue is the principal thing and in its name war must be waged against the passions, avarice, luxury, love, ambition.   So over and over the young preacher must repeat to his readers :

Come and learn, O miserable souls, and be instructed in the causes of things : learn what we are, and for what sort of lives we were born ; what place was assigned to us at the start ; how to round the turning-post gently, and from what point to begin the turn ; what limit should be placed on wealth ; what prayers may rightfully be offered ; what good there is in fresh-minted coin ; how much should be spent on country and kin ; what part

[3] J. Conington, *The Satires of A. Persius Flaccus,* Oxford, 1874, pp. xiii, 32–33.   [4] For a presentation of the opposite view, see Pretor, *op. cit.,* pp. xiii–xvii.

God has ordered you to play, and at what point of the human commonwealth you have been stationed. Learn these things.

discite et, o miseri, causas cognoscite rerum :
quid sumus et quidnam victuri gignimur, ordo
quis datus aut metae qua mollis flexus et unde,
quis modus argento, quid fas optare, quid asper
utile nummus habet, patriae carisque propinquis
quantum elargiri deceat, quem te deus esse
iussit et humana qua parte locatus es in re ;
disce.[5]

This fervor for the Stoic faith had its corollaries in religious ideas.   In the Stoic pantheistic conception of god, the old Roman idea of prayer as barter had to be discarded.   The man imbued with Stoicism will not crave wealth or material blessings, neither will he ask the gods for them.   Moreover, he will not, conceiving his god in his own faulty image, offer him in exchange gifts of incense and sacrifice as though deity craved delights of the senses.   Imagine offering to Jupiter, the oily entrails of a victim ! [6]

O Souls bowed down to earth, and void of all heavenly thoughts !   What avails it to bring our ideas into the temples, and to infer from this sinful flesh of ours what is pleasing to the gods ? . . . Nay rather let us offer to the gods . . . a heart rightly attuned towards God and man ; a mind pure in its inner depths, and a soul steeped in nobleness and honour.   Give me these to offer in the temples, and a handful of corn shall win my prayer for me !

O curvae in terris animae et caelestium inanes !
quid iuvat hoc, templis nostros immittere mores
et bona dis ex hac scelerata ducere pulpa ? . . .
quin damus id superis : . . .
compositum ius fasque animo sanctosque recessus
mentis et incoctum generoso pectus honesto.
haec cedo ut admoveam templis, et farre litabo.[7]

[5] *Sat.* III. 66–73, translated by G. G. Ramsay in *The Loeb Classical Library.*

[6] *Sat.* II.

[7] *Sat.* II. 61–75 (in part), translated by G. G. Ramsay in *The Loeb Classical Library.*

Something of this Stoic austerity and unworldliness helped predetermine Persius' literary standards. His greatest originality appears in his satire of literature. Here in an age when writing was fashionable and little scribblers imitated the emperor's effusions, a bold satirist had ample scope in deriding silly trivialities and senseless bombast. Persius had both the courage and the taste to undertake such criticism. His methods of attack will be shown in the study of his anecdotes : their pictures of *recitationes,* their revelation of what poor critics flattering dinner-guests or dependent clients make. But here in introduction we must only mention Persius' literary forbears and the reasons for his adopting the form of satire to convey his message.

The *Life* records that as soon as Persius was done with school and teachers, on reading the tenth book of Lucilius he had a passionate desire to compose Satires. Lucilius then, the censorious critic of the Republic, was the determining factor in the selection of his form. A far more potent influence in his development of his genre was however Horace. The six Satires are impregnated with Horace's ethical themes and colored by Horace's style. Indeed as one Horatian phrase follows another in Persius' lines, his poetry seems a sort of renaissance cento made up of the *curiosa felicitas* of the great Venusian. What prevents Persius' Satires from being mere imitation is that he has fused all his borrowed material in the single-mindedness of his Stoicism until it is transformed into the white light of a great faith. Intermingled too with Horatian expression are influences of Greek Comedy, of Roman Comedy, and of the diatribes of the Cynic preachers. And all this flotsam and jetsam comes out clothed in motley, for even the language though predominantly Horatian holds in solution archaic tags, slang of the streets, philosophic terms.   It is this mixture of elements which produces often tantalizing obscurity of expression.

Before we are prepared to read the anecdotes in Persius, we must do what we have done in each essay : let the author himself present his own theory of his poetry.   Persius' own comments on his satire and its themes are presented in a Prologue and in Satires I and V.   Unlike the rest of his poems which are in hexameters the Prologue is written in scazons.   The unique use of this metre to open the book of Satires and to introduce Persius' revolt against the poetic pretensions of his time bears the stamp of Lucilian coinage, for as Duff has observed : "The scazons introduced by Petronius in the *Satyricon* as a kind of Lucilian imitation lend color to the idea that Lucilius' influence acted upon the so-called *Prologus* in the same meter." [8]

Persius' scazons are full of self-irony about poetry.

"I am not a real poet," he declares, "for I never drank from the spring of the Nag Pegasus ; I never dreamed on two-peaked Parnassus.   I give up the Maids of Helicon, the Muses, and Peirene's spring to the old bards who are now just ivy-crowned busts.   I myself am a mere outsider to the guild of poets, a *semipaganus,* for I was never taught to sing by the Belly,

that master of art and of genius the purveyor,

magister artis ingenique largitor,

which taught the parrot his χαîρε and the magpies our words !"

Thus ironically Persius avers that poverty never tuned his lyre for nothings or taught him parrot-like imitativeness.   He revolts against all the high-sounding mythology of poetic inspiration from the true, the blushful Hippocrene and from Peirene's blanching waters.   He will

[8] *Satyricon,* 4 ; J. Wight Duff, *Roman Satire,* Berkeley, California, 1936, p. 115.

stand outside all professional guilds of poets and dare to be himself.

Satire I is Persius' apologia for writing satire. It is part of the great Roman tradition, for it begins with a quotation from Lucilius, it is full of phrases from Horace, it was the model for Juvenal's first Satire. In form, it is a dialogue between Persius and a fictitious interlocutor. Persius confides to this *auditor* or *monitor* that there is something which he must announce to Rome. He hints his secret first in line eight, finally reveals it in line one hundred and twenty-one :

> auriculas asini quis non habet ?

> What man is there who has not asses' ears ?

On that keynote, he develops his charges against literature. First, writers of both prose and poetry aim primarily at notoriety : [9]

> Great god ! And so your knowledge goes for naught
> Unless another knows you have knowledge got !

> O mores, usque adeone
> scire tuum nihil est, nisi te scire hoc sciat alter ?

To develop this theme of the vanities of would-be literary men, he paints a picture of a *recitatio* in which he satirizes self-satisfied authors : [10]

> We seclude ourselves and write something in the grand style, one in prose, one in poetry, something that makes the lungs distend to read. Yet read this stuff some day you will to the people. You'll dress all up in a fine new toga white, your birthday sardonyx on your finger. You'll take your seat on a high throne, gargle a bit to lubricate your vocal chords, and then assume the rakish gleam in the eye that starts the titillations of the crowd !

The themes of such poets are salacious old myths with a sentimental tinge, a story of Phyllis or Hypsipyle. They

[9] *Sat.* I. 26–27.   [10] *Sat.* I. 13–18.

write in a grandiloquent style with no power to describe real life. Their poems are full of rhetoric, not art, abounding as they do in polished antitheses and learned figures of speech. Their feeling, moreover, is not sincere, yet the man who will wish to bow me down with his sad plaint must by his own true tears beget tears.

The interlocutor protesting that at least the new poets have achieved charm and polish recites a specimen of such frothy stuff. Then at Persius' request he produces also an example of the sentimental, languishing type. Persius denounces both in violent invectives. He then proclaims his own creed : he will follow the frank, fearless satire of Lucilius and Horace ; he will write for those who have understood the spirit of the old Attic Comedy of Cratinus, Eupolis and the grand old man, Aristophanes. So again to his theme :

> auriculas asini quis non habet ?

His subjects and his style are announced more explicitly in Satire V. This is the most warm-hearted of Persius' Satires, for it is full of devotion to his guide, philosopher and friend, Lucius Annaeus Cornutus. Its composition contains a mixture of Stoic themes, Horace's satire (particularly Sat. II. 7), a scene from a comedy of Menander worked over by Terence and some autobiography. Its theme is that all men are slaves and the great need of mankind is true liberty. In it Persius attacks the grandiose themes of moderns who wish to write epics or sad tragedies on frightful old myths, the cannibalic banquets of Tereus or Thyestes. With such subjects he contrasts everyday themes, the dinners of the poor, the faults of men. He compares too the grand style of the pretentious with the language of every day which the true poet will use. He makes Cornutus say to him : [11]

[11] *Sat.* V. 13-15.

You do not try to puff out your cheeks, till they are deflated in a 'Plop.' You seek the words of every day, but cunning are in pointed phrasing, polished but plain in tone.

nec scloppo tumidas intendis rumpere buccas.
verba togae sequeris iunctura callidus acri,
ore teres modico.

It is thus that Persius by his self-criticism leads us to the consideration of the little stories which he tells to drive his great truths home.

In noting the types of anecdotes which he uses we are not surprised that among them are no myths at all. Unlike Horace, he seldom resorts to fable. His stories are sown with a sparing hand, but they are effectively told.

One group consists of stories of childhood and education which seems to have an autobiographical flavor. Once his *alter ego* accuses him of being a baby : [12]

For like a little prince you wish your food cut small and, angry, shut your ears to mamma's lullaby.

et similis regum pueris pappare minutum
poscis et iratus mammae lallare recusas.

In another passage where Persius is discussing foolish prayers, he tells a story of charms performed over a child by his grandmother or aunt : [13]

Just look! A granny or an auntie who fears the gods takes baby out of his bed. With middle finger she daubs lustral spittle on his forehead and drooling lips, for she knows how to avert the evil eye. Then she dandles the thin young hopeful in her arms and by her prayers ordains him for the estates of Licinus or Crassus' palace. And she prays : 'May king and queen wish him for son-in-law! May the girls rush after him! May his path be roses, roses all the way!' To no such nurse do I e'er commit my prayers.

Again in a passage, entitled by Gildersleeve "Boys will be boys," Persius describes his resentment of the education

[12] *Sat.* III. 17–18.   [13] *Sat.* II. 31–39.

of the rhetorical schools and his fondness for games of dice, marbles and top : [14]

> Often as a lad I remember I rubbed my eyes with olive oil if I did not wish to recite the lofty speech of Cato on the eve of suicide, a speech that my crazy teacher would be sure to praise, which father would bring all his friends to hear while he sweat pride. And rightly did I so, for my greatest wish was knowing what the highest throw of the dice would give me, what the lowest cost ; how to get my marbles neatly into the little hole and lash the top more rapidly than any other boy.

There are very few anecdotes about historical characters and these are probably stock examples from the training of the rhetorical schools. Two are merely alluded to as proof that fear is the greatest punishment : the brazen bull of Phalaris, the hair-suspended sword over the head of Damocles.[15] An anecdotal character sketch of Alcibiades is written as a series of questions proposed to him by Socrates. The philosopher interrogates Alcibiades on what justice is ; on what is the greatest good. His questions reveal Alcibiades' lack of judgment, his effeminacy, his self-satisfaction. After the character sketch comes the moral with an allusion to the fable of the two wallets : [16]

> Ah ! No one tries to descend into himself !
> Each looks at the wallet on the back ahead.
>
> ut nemo in sese temptat descendere, nemo,
> sed praecedenti spectatur mantica tergo !

This anecdote seems to me to be what it purports to be : Socrates' instruction of his beloved wastrel, Alcibiades. As a vignette of Greek education it is a companion piece to the snapshot of Roman education in the rhetorical schools.[17] Alcibiades and young Nero had the faults of youth in common.[18] But it seems far-fetched to make this

---

[14] *Sat.* III. 44–51.
[15] *Sat.* III. 39–41.
[16] *Sat.* IV. 1–24.

[17] *Sat.* III. 44–51.
[18] See Pretor, *op. cit.*, pp. xvi–xvii.

exemplum of the young Greek gallant a covert criticism
of the emperor. Then Socrates would have to represent
Seneca and since Persius did not find Seneca *simpatico,* he
would hardly have cast Lucan's uncle in so distinguished
a rôle. Alcibiades made such a palpable moral lesson for
the young that he was undoubtedly one of the stock examples of the schools. The material is taken from the
Platonic dialogue called the *First Alcibiades* and some of
the words from a speech in the *Symposium.*[19]

The dialogue with Alcibiades has an ethical point and
so is associated with a group of anecdotes portraying types
of characters from contemporary life. One is a thumb-
nail sketch of a sick glutton.[20] He consults a doctor, follows his directions for only three nights, then stuffs and
drinks again and after dinner dies at the baths. The story
is told rapidly with reminiscences of Horace, conversation
and disgusting realism. A similar ethical anecdote is a
vignette of the sordid miser, Ventidius.[21] He drinks wine
without wiping off the jar before he pours it out, chews up
an onion skin and all and guzzles in dregs of wine turned
vinegar.

Several philosophical anecdotes illustrate the need of liberty by showing different types of men who are not free.[22]
The praetor's rod by its tap may make a freedman out of
a slave but it does not give him true freedom. This point
is made by a description of the manumission of a slave,
Dama, and of the new freedman's power.

That the avaricious man is not free is proved by a dialogue between Avarice, *avaritia,* and the Avaricious Man,
avarus, with the moral : "Give up the hunt for wealth ;
free yourself."

[19] p. 216, A. See John Conington,
op. cit., p. 72.
[20] *Sat.* III. 88–106.
[21] *Sat.* IV. 23–32.

[22] *Sat.* V. 73–82, 151–53, 161–75.
The prose translations are by G. G.
Ramsay in *The Loeb Classical Li-
brary.*

Indulge your soul !   And let us gather joys.
Today you live, but when tomorrow comes,
You will be ashes, shade, a tale that is told.
So live with eye on death.   The hour flees.
The word I speak is now a moment gone.

indulge genio, carpamus dulcia, nostrum est
quod vivis, cinis et manes et fabula fies.
vive memor leti, fugit hora, hoc quod loquor inde est.

Another type of man who is a slave is the roué who tries
to break away from his mistress and reform, but cannot
liberate himself.   This is related as a dialogue between
Charestratus and the slave, Davus.   The dialogue is taken
from the *Eunuchus* of Menander as translated by Terence,
but the names used are from the Greek instead of the
Phaedria and Parmenio of Terence.

"Here, Davus, quick !   I am in real earnest ; I mean to bring
my past follies to an end."   So says Chaerestratus, biting his nails
to the quick.   "What ?   Am I to be a stumbling block and a
scandal to my excellent relations ?   Am I to lose alike my patri-
mony and my character by singing drunken songs, with my torch
put out, before my mistress's dripping door ?"   "Bravo ! my
young sir.   Show your good sense, and slay a lamb to the Pro-
tecting Deities !"   "But do you think, Davus, that she will cry
if I leave her ?"   "You're just playing the fool !   And won't
you be catching it, my boy, with her red slipper, just to teach
you not to jib or to gnaw at the tight-drawn meshes !   At one
moment you're all bluster and indignation ; next moment, if she
call you back, you'll be saying, 'What *am* I to do ?   Am I not to
go to her even now, when she sends for me, and actually implores
me to return ?'   No, no, say I, not even now, if once you have
got away from her entire and heart-whole."   Here, here is the
freedom we are looking for, not in the stick brandished by that
nincompoop of a lictor.

One more ethical anecdote should be mentioned.   This
is not on liberty, but on the proper use of wealth.[23]   The
conflict involved is expressed in epigrams :

[23] *Sat.* VI. 22–42, translated by G. G. Ramsay in *The Loeb Classical Library.*

I will enjoy, I will enjoy !

utar ego, utar,

and

but duty calls,

at vocat officium.

Here Duty summons the Wealthy Man to succor a friend
in distress, not to hoard for an heir.   The anecdotal description of the poor, shipwrecked friend is very pitiful in
its realism.

He is clutching hold of the rocks of Bruttium, all his goods and
his unheeded prayers sunk in the Ionian Sea ; he himself lies upon
the shore, the great Gods from the ship's poop beside him ; the
gulls are by this time flocking to the shattered timbers.

But if you help him, your heir will declare you have
diminished his property.   And some stupid Bestius will
argue that this is just the sort of foolish extravagance that
Greek philosophers have taught men !   Such an ironic
reductio ad absurdum stabs into the reader's mind the
Satire's point :

Sell not your soul for gain.

This review of Persius' use of anecdotes has inevitably
occupied less space than the introduction to them.   An
author whose work consists of only six Satires amounting
to six hundred and fifty hexameters and who wrote these
in the plain style would not exhibit many *lumina* and
ornamenta.   He is consistent in his use of them with his
principles for his satire.   Their spirit is the frankness of
the old Attic Comedy, Lucilius and Horace.   His subjects
are never myths, but life itself and the follies of mankind.
These themes are conditioned by his ardor for Stoicism
which supplied him with texts of virtue, true liberty, the
curses of ignorance, superstition, passion and wealth.   Inevitably since he was more a preacher than a poet his anecdotes took on the nature of moral stories, not of ornaments,

and were used to convey the ethical and religious tenets of his philosophical school.

His style is never grand but the plain style of every day. Horace is constantly his model in themes as well as in phraseology. Indeed his elaborate imitations of Horace combine with the language of the rhetorical and philosophical schools and the realistic slang of the streets to produce at times a challenging obscurity. This appears less in his *exempla* with their pointed morals than in his running descriptions. Some of his anecdotes are merely hinted in allusions. Others are related in brief, pungent character sketches. In them he uses quotations from Plato, Terence, Lucilius, and Horace as well as Horace's devices of dialogue, of fictitious interlocutor, of a telling *sententia* to point a moral. He shows more than does Horace the effect of his training in the schools. And in this particular as well as in the passionate nature of his satire he is a vital link between Horace and Juvenal.

Much of his poetry is explained by his life. Having lost his father at the age of six he was brought up by his mother, aunt and sister towards whom he showed exemplary devotion. Education in Volaterrae till twelve and in Rome under famous rhetoricians till sixteen never woke him up. Then the influence of a great teacher made a man and a Stoic of him. His poetry is the revolt of youth against the superstitions of women, the cant of the schools, the conventions of society, the superstitions of religion. His thought is dominated by a Stoic fervor for uprightness, freedom, integrity. Had he lived longer his style might have been as purified as his creed. Yet these six Satires deserve the encomia of his contemporaries and of ancient critics. Lucan said that Persius' work was true poetry, his own mere play (illa esse vera poemata, sua ludos). Quintilian stated that Persius had won much true glory although he wrote only one book.[24]   The Christian fathers, Lactantius, Augustine, and especially Jerome, cherished him for his ethical seriousness, his sternness in correcting morals and his *anima naturaliter Christiana.*

[24] Quintilian, *I. O.,* X. 1, 94.

VIII

THE BITTER STORIES OF THE SATIRIST JUVENAL

THE Age of Domitian is the background for Juvenal's Satires though like Tacitus he kept silent during those dire times, publishing nothing until after the emperor's death.[1] Silence was necessary, for as the historian records, rage was vented not merely upon authors, but upon their books so that works of distinction and genius were burned in the assembly and in the Forum ; rulers thought forsooth that by that fire the voice of the Roman people, the liberty of the senate and the conscience of the human race could be destroyed. And more, they drove into exile professors of philosophy and all their knowledge, that nowhere might the dignity of truth confront themselves.[2] Juvenal's famous line,

> It is difficult not to write satire,
>
> difficile est saturam non scribere,[3]

is more understandable when one reads Tacitus' account of the period which they had endured : [4]

Sacred rites were defiled ; there were adulteries in high places. The sea was filled with exiles, its cliffs made foul with the bodies of the dead. In Rome there was more awful cruelty. High birth, wealth, the refusal or acceptance of office — all gave ground for

---

[1] Tacitus, *Agric.* 3.
[2] Tac. *Agric.* 2.
[3] Juvenal, *Sat.* I. 30.

[4] Tac. *Hist.*, I, 2–3, translated by Clifford H. Moore in *The Loeb Classical Library.*

accusations, and virtues caused the surest ruin. The rewards of the informers were no less hateful than their crimes ; for some, gaining priesthoods and consulships as spoils, others, obtaining positions as imperial agents and secret influence at court, robbed and ruined without limit, inspiring universal hatred and terror. Slaves were corrupted against their masters, freedmen against their patrons ; and those who had no enemy were crushed by their friends.

Yet this age was not so barren of virtue that it did not display noble examples. Mothers accompanied their children in flight ; wives followed their husbands into exile ; relatives displayed courage, sons-in-law firmness, slaves a fidelity which defied even torture. Eminent men met the last necessity with fortitude, rivalling in their end the glorious deaths of antiquity.

Under such tyranny, a Stoic, Thrasea Paetus, opened his veins and as the blood gushed forth, announced to the quaestor : "I am offering a libation to Jupiter, the Liberator. Look at me, young man . . . for you have been born in such times that you need to strengthen your soul by examples of fortitude." [5] After Domitian was dead, the historian could take up his work in the rare felicity of an age when man might feel what he wished and say what he felt.[6] And the satirist, Juvenal, could give free play to his *ira* and his *indignatio*.[7]

It was Domitian that made Tacitus and Juvenal great moralists who taught by *acria exempla* and *bona exempla* [8] of famous words and deeds.

It is natural though disappointing to find, therefore, the early life of Juvenal wrapped in obscurity. On account of what Highet calls "his proud or timid affectation of anonymity," [9] in Juvenal the autobiographical character of satire which made the life of Lucilius appear in his pages as though painted on a votive tablet,[10] has disappeared. Or rather, I should say, the realistic autobiography of facts

[5] Tac. *Ann.* XVI. 35.
[6] Tac. *Hist.* I. 1.
[7] Juv. *Sat.* I. 45 and 79.
[8] Juv. *Sat.* XIV. 322 ; Tac. *Hist.* I. 3.

[9] Gilbert Highet, "The Life of Juvenal," *T.P.A.P.A.* 68, 1937, p. 480.
[10] Horace, *Sat.* II. 1, 33-35.

has been succeeded by an impressionistic autobiography of personality.   The actual information which Juvenal's Satires give about himself is very scanty, and he says nothing about his youth.   His life has to be reconstructed from a few references in his poems, the testimony of other ancient authors, the evidence of an incomplete inscription, now lost, and the sifted out agreement of the many unreliable *Vitae* of the scholiasts.   Out of this fragmentary and inconclusive material Gilbert Highet has recently built with careful scholarship a life which may well serve as a working hypothesis for the study of Juvenal's poems.[11]

Juvenal was born free, about 55 A.D., and came from Aquinum. After receiving a good education, he successfully applied to the imperial government for admission to the equestrian rank and career.   During or after his service as commander of an auxiliary cohort, he dedicated a shrine to Ceres in his native town, and was given the highest honours Aquinum could bestow.   When his service in the cohort was over, he was not promoted.   He lived in Rome during the first part of Domitian's reign, and cultivated the nobles who might have helped, but they were uninterested or unsuccessful.

Meanwhile, he saw that court favourites were able to promote their friends, and that merit, in Rome, did not mean success.   He lingered on in Rome for some years, practising literature in a dilettante way, and waiting.   Then he wrote a short satire on the advancement of the unworthy, and used the name of Paris, dead in disgrace some eight or nine years since, as an example.   The suspicious Domitian took this as a covert attack on the probity of his administration, and exiled Juvenal to Egypt, confiscating all his considerable property.

When he returned, he was a middle-aged man, penniless and without prospects.   He lived for some years as a client of the rich, writing poetry which had small success.   His satires were published by books : I and II under Trajan, III, IV, and V under Hadrian.   In late middle life, he inherited or earned some property, which enabled him to end his days in comparative comfort, so that he died less bitterly than he had lived.   His last book of satires may have been published by friends after death.

There are three stages in that reconstruction.   The first two

11 Highet, *op. cit.*, pp. 480–506.

need not be accepted. The officer who erected the lost inscription may well have been another Juvenal, and the tradition of the exile might be a scholiast's invention ; but at least the reconstruction is possible. What is certain and permanent in the satires is the enduring hate and fear of Domitian, and the deep contempt for humanity and its standards, which inspire them throughout, and for which this reconstruction would supply a personal motive.

From the Satires themselves other striking features in the total personality of the man emerge. His education had clearly culminated in the rhetorical schools of Rome, not in mellowing Athens as Horace's did. Partly because of his mastery of rhetoric, partly because of the fierce indignation which moved his quill, he broke with the traditional use of the conversational tone of satire and wrote in the grand style. His Roman education and his limited travels made him peculiarly nationalistic in his point of view so he poses as a foe to all foreigners in Rome, especially the Greeks. But his moral indignation rages most fiercely against the Romans who have betrayed the *mos maiorum,* the fine traditions of their Republican ancestors and ideals.

Before we reconstruct Juvenal's literary autobiography from his Satires, a foundation for it must be laid by assembling his comments on Roman education to show what he thought of his own. The *Vita* of Probus tells us that Juvenal practised declamation until about middle age more for the sake of amusement than as a preparation for teaching in a school or pleading in the Forum. Juvenal himself in his great preface informs us that he too drew back his hand from the teacher's ferule in the rhetorical schools and he gives us vivid accounts of the practice speeches which the pupils there were taught to compose and deliver : *suasoriae* in which Sulla was advised to abandon politics and sleep well [12] or dire Hannibal was counseled as to whether

[12] Juv. *Sat.* I. 15–17.

after his victory at Cannae he should march straight on Rome ; *controversiae,* imaginary civil cases on rape, poisoning and wicked and ungrateful husbands.   Juvenal's sympathy goes out to the teacher who must have an iron heart to hear his many pupils slay cruel tyrants over and over, each one repeating the same theme in the same words until the wretched pedagogue perishes from the cabbage crammed down his throat again and again.[13]

And the *rhetor* is not considered worthy of his hire, for all wish to learn but no one wishes to pay.   A noble will spend fortunes on baths, porticoes, banquet halls, but two thousand sesterces are enough for the great Quintilian's salary.   A father will spend a fortune on everything but his son !   Many have repented of the professor's useless and unremunerated chair.

> And one there was in Athens who was poor,
> And for a pension won the hemlock chill.
> Let the earth rest lightly on our sires, O Gods,
> Let fragrant crocus and eternal spring
> Bloom o'er their urns, for they alone did set
> The teacher in the sacred parent's place.[14]

So Juvenal, while he satirizes the faults of Roman education, exalts the teacher.   The name of Quintilian, the greatest of the rhetoricians, is often on his lips and without resentment he sorrowfully envies him the favor of Fortune which gave him wealth and made out of the *rhetor* a consul.[15]   Perhaps such political advancement was what Juvenal hoped from his practice of oratory referred to in the *Vita,* so that he envied Quintilian the political preferment which he himself never achieved.

I believe that in the same way he coveted, though he never says so, the education in Greece which Horace, one

---

[13] Juv. *Sat.* VII. 150–70.
[14] Juv. *Sat.* VII. 178–210.
[15] Juv. *Sat.* VII. 185–98.

of his admitted models, enjoyed.   Juvenal's virulent satire
of the Greeklings in Rome has outweighed in his readers'
minds his intense admiration for Greek literature, art and
philosophy.   Of course, his lurid painting of Grecized
Rome is unforgettable.   There simple rustics ape fantas-
tic Greeks.   And the Greek émigrés insinuate themselves
into the houses of the great and become their masters.
Chameleons, they change their character at your will.
They flatter, they act, they corrupt, they grab, and then
become informers.   Yet these perfumed Corinthians set
the fashion so that wanton women copy their language and
their love-making.   The satirist cannot endure this Rome
turned Greek.[16]

Juvenal, however, is full of reverence for the beauty of
Greek literature and myths.   The treasures of his poor
man's attic are divine Greek poems.[17]   At his ideal, simple
dinner the Iliad will be chanted.[18]   Although he denounces Greek myths as themes for poetry he draws several
of his *exempla* from them.[19]   He knows the value of works
of art by Parrhasius, Myron, Phidias, Mentor, Euphranor,
Polyclitus.[20]   He honors the Greek philosophers for their
lives and teaching : Socrates, Chrysippus, the nude Cynic
in his tub, the compassionate Pythagoras.[21]   Indeed Juvenal's satires are permeated by a sort of wistful worship of
the Greeks.   What he could not tolerate were the deca-
dents among them in Greece or in Rome and the ignorant
imitators of the true Greeks.   No poseurs or shams for
Juvenal.

The poet's *apologia* for his satire which constitutes his
first poem is now more comprehensible, read against our
working hypothesis of his life and our knowledge of his

[16] Juv. *Sat.* III. 58–125 ; VIII. 112–
15 ; VI. 184–99.

[17] Juv. *Sat.* III. 206–7.

[18] Juv. *Sat.* XI. 179–80.

[19] See *Satires* VI. and X.

[20] Juv. *Sat.* VIII. 98–107 ; III. 212–
22.

[21] Juv. *Sat.* XIII. 183–92 ; XIV. 308–
21 ; XV. 171–74.

relation to the education of the time.   The key-notes to
this *apologia* are his phrases already quoted,

difficile est saturam non scribere

and his *saeva indignatio*.   He begins with a dashing question :

What ?   All my days must I to bards give ear
And never sing ?

Then he attacks the second-rate versifiers who all day long
spout their epics and their tragedies at private readings so
that from the greatest and the smallest poet you hear the
same hackneyed myths.   Juvenal has had the same education as these poetasters, but he is not going to rehash the
stories of Hercules or Diomedes, of the bellowing in the
labyrinth, of the flying Daedalus and the lad who fell into
the sea, of Achilles, of Hylas, even of Aeneas and Turnus.
His heart burns with rage when he sees in Rome an ef-
feminate eunuch marrying, a barber turned into a millionaire, an Egyptian slave transformed into a knight, an informer who has ruined his patron.   These are the themes
which force him to write satire.

Of course some of these tales of everyday life are as
marvellous as the old myths.   But even Ulysses when he
was relating his own experiences to the astonished Alcinous, moved some of his hearers to anger and derision as
if he were a lying story-teller, *mendax aretalogus*.[22]   But,
for all that, Juvenal is going to tell his "true stories" and
he invokes the Muses to aid him :

Begin, Calliope.   Now we may take our seats.   No song is to
be sung.   A true tale will be told.   Start the narration, maids of
Pieria !

incipe, **Calliope**.   licet et considere, non est
cantandum, res vera agitur.   narrate, puellae
Pierides.[23]

[22] Juv. *Sat*. XV. 13–16.   [23] Juv. *Sat*. IV. 34–36.

Whate'er men do, their prayers, their fears, their wrath,
Their lust and joys, their runnings to and fro,
Shall make the medley of my little book.

quidquid agunt homines, votum timor ira voluptas
gaudia discursus, nostri farrago libelli est.[24]

The poet is aware that the traditional style for the handling of the subjects of satire is the plain style. Horace had dubbed his Satires 'conversations,' *sermones,* and had declared that the Muse who inspired them was pedestrian and no true critic would ever call them poetry.[25] But Juvenal affirms that he sometimes needs even the style of tragedy in his satire of real life to fit his themes, for example for the woman poisoner who kills the children of her husband's concubine, a veritable Medea.[26]

Am I inventing these stories ? Is my satire donning the high cothurn of tragedy ? Having gone beyond the limits and laws of previous satirists am I raving through a song in the grand style of a Sophocles, a song unknown to the Rutulian hills and the skies of Latium ? Would that I were not telling true stories !

His intense horror at the facts of life, his indignation, forced Juvenal to adopt the grand style, the *os magna sonaturum,* which Horace rejected for his *sermones.* Since, however, his chosen medium was satire, its conventional metre, hexameter, forced him to the grand style, not of tragedy, but of epic. And we shall find him using constantly epic diction, epic coloring, even some of the despised epic myths both in serious imitation of epic narrative and in conscious parody of it.[27]

His emotional reaction to the vices of his age conditioned also the function of his stories. They are used to teach

[24] Juv. *Sat.* I. 85–86.
[25] Hor. *Sat.* I. 4, 42–48 ; *Ep.* II. 1, 250–51 ; *Sat.* II. 6, 17.
[26] Juv. *Sat.* VI. 634–38.

[27] Inez G. Scott, "The Grand Style in the Satires of Juvenal," in *Smith College Classical Studies,* no. 8, May, 1927, Northampton, Mass.

moral lessons.   Juvenal himself acknowledges their purpose.   Once when he has told a pair of stories on the old
theme of the rhetoricians, "Rich Man Poor Man," about
the millionaire Licinus and the nude Cynic in his tub, he
asks his fictitious interlocutor with whom he is arguing for
the simple life,

Do I seem to force you to a corner by bitter examples ?

acribus exemplis videor te cludere ? [28]

Juvenal takes us into his confidence not only about his
subject matter, his style, his purpose, but also about his
sources and his methods of work.   Trained in the schools
of the rhetoricians, he has chosen satire for his medium and
he has decided to follow two distinguished models.   One
is the great child of Aurunca, Lucilius, the other the one
who threw the light of his Venusian lamp upon the world,
Horatius Flaccus.[29]   With such training and such proto-
types, he will stand at the cross-roads and take notes on
large wax tablets about the ridiculous *homunculi* who
pass.   For safety, since Lucilius' daring sword-thrusts
aroused anger, he would better write of men dead and gone
whose ashes are buried by the Flaminian and the Latin
Roads.[30]   With this announcement which dimly veils the
fact that he is harking back to the age of Domitian, Juvenal concludes his Prologue Satire in defence of satire.

In the telling of his stories of the past, Juvenal employs
varied methods.   One is the use of *exempla* as illustrations where a familiar story is not told, but only alluded
to.   The story is so famous that it is recaptured for the
imagination by a few significant words.   As quotations
"in solution" challenge the reader's knowledge, so suggested stories demand attention and memory for their connotation.   This drawing on the storehouse of the reader's

28 Juv. *Sat.* XIV. 322.   30 Juv. *Sat.* I. 63–72, 165–71.
29 Juv. *Sat.* I. 19–21, 51–52.

mind permits the amplification of the grand style by the presentation of *exempla* in a long series which has tremendous accumulative effect. This is the method used in both the tenth and sixth Satires.

The tenth is perhaps the most logically perfect in structure of all Juvenal's poems. This discussion of "the Vanity of Human Wishes" starts with the theme to which it swings back in full circle at the end. First observe that few men can distinguish true blessings : reason does not cause our fears or our desires. Reflect on the ruinous ambitions of mankind. Then, finally, leave life's direction to the gods, who will give us what is best instead of what is pleasing. Man can give himself only this : the certainty that the one path to the life of peace is the highway of virtue.

Within this frame are fitted the *exempla* of the vain ambitions of men. But first, the chief desire of all, wealth, is not portrayed in concrete pictures of past men in the mad race for it, but by the effect of the spectacle of that race on two Greek philosophers, Heraclitus who wept every time he stepped across his threshold into the world of men, Democritus who at every meeting with them found material for laughter in their cares, their joys, yes, even in their tears.

With the easy censorship of Democritus' laughter at desire for wealth in mind, Juvenal proceeds to portray the other ambitions of men by rich allusions to great names. Political power which caused great envy overthrew Sejanus, Crassus, Pompey, Julius Caesar. Eloquence caused the destruction of two great orators, Cicero and Demosthenes. War trophies, military glory raised Hannibal, Alexander and Xerxes to the pinnacle of fame but death showed how small their bodies were. Long life proved no blessing to Nestor, Priam, Marius, Pompey and beauty caused the fateful end of Lucretia, Hippolytus, Bellerophon, Silius. Each name in this pageant of foredone ghosts awakes startled memories.

But a mere list would be colorless so pregnant phrases suggest details and at times the procession halts as if the eyes and mind of the spectator needed more time to take in the dreadful realism of some scene reproduced on the float that passes. Thus the series is broken and enriched by the stories of Sejanus, of Hannibal, of Silius.

We see the bronze equestrian statue of Tiberius' favorite, Sejanus, hurled into the furnace and from that face, the second in the whole world, pots, pans, and pails being fashioned. We see the corpse of Sejanus dragged along the streets by a hook, and the populace of Rome, which always follows fortune and hates the damned, rushing to kick the body on the river bank to prove they are with the government. No one now remembers what Sejanus' great wealth was, what his high position as guardian of the emperor.

Or weigh Hannibal ! How many pounds will you find in the greatest of generals ? Yet this is he who was not stayed by Africa, the Nile, the Aethiopians, or Spain. Nature set against him the Alps and their snows. He split the rocks, he burst the mountain with vinegar, and marched on his way to Rome. What a picture the one-eyed dux made, riding on his elephant ! Then what was his end ? Exile, clientship to a proud eastern monarch, at last the poison in his little ring !

Now look again ! This handsome, young patrician, Silius, the wife of Caesar has decided to wed. Decked in her marriage veil, she waits for her lover beside the bridal couch erected openly in the garden. All know the scandal but the emperor. Yet soon he will and in that fair white neck of Silius will be plunged a sword.

These three scenes from Satire X show how dramatically Juvenal employs every rhetorical device to make his *exempla* telling and how he revels in that feature of the grand style which is called "imagery," *visiones*, φαντασίαι, defined by Longinus as the "describing what is absent or only imaginary as if it were actually present to the sight." [31]

The use of anecdotes in Satire VI, "The Legend of Bad Women," might be analyzed in the same way. Juvenal's misogyny, which in all the great herds of women does not see one good, finds expression in the same sort of amplification by a long series of vivid examples, by the same imagery of living pictures, by the rhetorical devices of hyperbole, apostrophe, rhetorical question, antithesis. But the length of the poem (661 lines) has made the style more rambling and the structure less closely knit. The redundancy of illustration, the lack of discrimination between different types of "new" women, the savagery of attack combine to diminish the effectiveness of the satire as a whole. Individual anecdotes however are memorable character sketches.

Both in these two Satires (X and VI) and in others where a long series of anecdotes is not presented, short stories are told tersely to point a moral. Their sources are many: mythology, history, contemporary life.

Typical of the use of mythology is the introduction of the myth of Niobe to illustrate pride in women. She is paired with Cornelia, mother of the Gracchi, who counted the triumphs of her ancestors, the Scipios, among the riches of her dowry. The story of Niobe and her fatal boast about her six sons and her six daughters is told from the point of view of their father: [32]

"Spare them, I beg, Apollo: O Goddess, put away your arrows. My children have done nothing. Kill their

<hr />

[31] Inez G. Scott, *op. cit.*, pp. 20–21.   [32] Juv. *Sat.* VI. 172–77.

mother," cried Amphion.   But Apollo drew his bow and
Niobe buried her herd of children and their sire too be-
cause she thought herself more famous for her family than
Latona and more fecund than the white sow of Alba.

The anecdote told by allusion and a single speech from
the husband's viewpoint clinches Juvenal's argument
against woman's pride.

Tiny historical vignettes convey in a few lines the poverty of writers.   How can Rubrenus Lappa write as great
tragedies as the ancients when he has to pawn his play
Atreus to buy his dishes and his cloak ? [33]   The poet Statius draws great crowds when he gives a reading of his
beloved *Thebais* and wins by its charm wild applause.
Yet afterwards he will starve unless he sells his virgin *Agave*
to Paris, the pantomimist.[34]

Many of the anecdotes of contemporary life turn on the
hard lot of poverty which makes men ridiculous.   The
contrast between the rich and the poor is of course a theme
taken straight from the *controversiae* of the rhetorical
schools as many of the cases in Seneca and the pseudo-
Quintilian show.   But Juvenal added to the rhetoric of
the schools his keen observation of conditions in his times
and his personal experiences.

Brief acrid comments epigrammatize the heartlessness
of the rich.   One man loses in gambling a hundred thousand sesterces, but cannot afford to give a tunic to his shiv-
ering slave.[35]   Numitor, unfortunate fellow, has nothing
to give a friend, but he keeps a mistress and feeds vast
amounts of meat to his tame lion.[36]   Then if disaster
comes to poor and rich alike, to him that hath shall be
given.   If fire destroys the attic in which Codrus lodged,
to be sure he loses only his bed, his table with six plates
and one goblet, an old box holding some divine Greek

[33] Juv. *Sat.* VII. 72-73.   [35] Juv. *Sat.* I. 92-93.
[34] Juv. *Sat.* VII. 81-87.   [36] Juv. *Sat.* VII. 74-78.

poems.   Codrus had nothing to be sure, but he lost that nothing !   And this crowns his misery, that when he is naked, begging bread, no one will aid him with food, bed or kindness.   But when the palace of Asturicus burns down, all the city puts on mourning.   Men rush to offer him gleaming statues, books, money to replace his losses. And at the end he's so much better off, that some think he set his house on fire ! [37]

The most detailed anecdote about the poor man's life is on his struggle for the dole.   This picture of "Morning Calls on a Rich Patron" might be a painting by Pieter Bruegel, the Elder : so rich is it in figures and in details. The noble opens his door and anxiously inspects the mob of high and low.   He bids his heralds summon the nobles first, crying : "Make way for the praetor, make way for the tribune."   A bold freedman protests : "I got here first. What if I was born near the Euphrates ?   Now I own five shops and have a larger income than any senator."   So tribunes must wait behind those who yesterday were slaves. Yet still they wait, for at the end of the year, they calculate with pleasure how much the dole adds to their income. To the poor who crowd with them to the patron's door the dole gives toga, shoes, bread, hearth-fire at home !   A crowd of litters is coming up.   A husband takes around on his calls a sick or pregnant wife.   Or, by a well-known trick, he talks to an empty litter with the curtains drawn : "My Galla's here.   Do let us go quickly.   Galla, put out your head.   Pray don't disturb her : she is resting !" [38]

Other themes developed by *exempla* of contemporary life are disgrace brought on old families by low acts and the lust and cruelty of women.   In Satire VIII whose theme is 'What use is there in family crests and fore-fathers ?' the consul Lateranus disgraces his ancestors by

[37] Juv. *Sat.* III. 197–222.   [38] Juv. *Sat.* I. 95–126.

driving his own mules and frequenting low taverns. Damasippus to retrieve his fortunes acts in a mime on the stage. And a Gracchus fights in the arena as a gladiator of the meanest type. So low are fallen nobles.[39]

The most vivid anecdotes about women come of course from Satire VI. Lust was never more unsparingly dealt with than in the stories of a senator's wife, Eppia, who ran away to Egypt with a gladiator and of the imperial harlot, Messalina, who left Claudius' bed to prostitute herself in a brothel.[40] The merciless and revolting realism of these stories conveys to the reader Juvenal's disgust.

The cruelty of women is pictured in miniatures where a whole story is suggested by a single action or a few quoted words. Here is a brief dialogue which betrays a woman's character : [41]

"Crucify that slave !" says the wife. "But what crime worthy of death has he committed ?" asks the husband ; "where are the witnesses ? Who informed against him ? Give him a hearing at least ; no delay can be too long when a man's life is at stake !" "What, you numskull ? You call a slave a man, do you ? He has done no wrong, you say ? Be it so ; but this is my will and my command : let my will be the voucher for the deed." Thus does she lord it over her husband.

Another woman, the athletic type, if her sleep is broken by a barking dog, has first the dog beaten, then his humble owner.[42] Another, a would-be beauty at her toilet, has her slave-girl flogged for a curl badly set, and sits making up her face or looking at a new dress while the flogging goes on.[43] The vitality of all these short stories of poverty, of disgrace, of lust, of cruelty comes from their unsparing realism and their vigorous bitterness. The moralist is a

[39] Juv. *Sat*. VIII. 146–210.
[40] Juv. *Sat*. VI. 82–132.
[41] Juv. *Sat*. VI. 219–24, translated by G. G. Ramsay in *The Loeb Classical Library*.
[42] Juv. *Sat*. VI. 413–33.
[43] Juv. *Sat*. VI. 474–511

Jeremiah : he is also the voice of one crying in the wilderness for reform.

Different from the long series of stories suggested rather than told and from the incidental anecdotes told for definite moral purpose are certain Satires which are each an anecdote in itself and each written as an epic parody. These are Satires IV, XII and XV.[44] The subject of Satire IV is the Council of great men called by Domitian to discuss the momentous problem of how to dispose of a huge fish which had been presented to the emperor. There is good evidence to support the theory that this Satire is a parody of a passage in a lost poem by Statius. the *Bellum Germanicum,* in which an imperial council meeting was described.[45] This contention is supported by the sustained epic style of the poem ; the mock heroic invocation of the muse Calliope ; the poetic descriptions of nature and of the time of year ; the epic circumlocutions to designate persons ; and grandiloquent descriptions. Virtually the whole Satire of 154 lines is composed in a mock heroic tone which heightens the absurdity of the imperial council's solemn discussion of what to do with a fish !

Around this subject and through this style, the most mordant wit plays. At Domitian's Alban citadel the excluded senators before his door watch the fish enter ! The fisherman presents his prize with the words : "Eat the rhombus preserved for your times ! The fish itself wished to be caught !" As Domitian (true cock of the walk) hears these words, his crest rises. When no platter can be found to suit the monster's size, the emperor calls a council of

---

[44] This discussion is based on Inez G. Scott, *op. cit.,* pp. 77–90.

[45] See Valla's quotation of four lines of Statius' poems and Buecheler's discussion, *Rhein. Mus.* 1884, p. 284.

nobles on whose faces is seen the pallor of their great and wretched friendship.

What a gathering it is ! Here is the gentle lawyer Pegasus who would remove in these dread times the sword from the hands of Justice. Here is Crispus whose nature and eloquence were mild for he knew the peril of the times. He never struck out against the current. He was not a citizen who could speak with freedom the words of his soul and stake his life on truth so he lived safe in that palace till he was eighty. Another came, prudent Veiento, a blind flatterer, a beggar courtier, only fit to run along by the chariots on the hill of Aricia and throw a beggar's kisses to the departing car. These and others like them are the senators, who solemnly discuss Domitian's small perplexity ! This same biting irony concludes the story :

Would that his majesty had devoted to such trifles as this those times of savagery in which he deprived the city of bright, glorious spirits with none to say him nay, none to take vengeance. He lived while his hands were dripping with the noble blood of the Lamiae. But when he began to terrorize the populace, the people killed him.

Satire XII is not a parody of any particular epic, but a general parody of an epic subject and the epic style of treatment of it. The occasion of the poem is the safe return of Juvenal's friend, Catullus, from a storm at sea and the theme of the narrative is the storm. Juvenal himself ironically points us to his parody of epic tradition when he begins his description :

Everything happened in the same way and with as much violence as in a storm in a poem.

omnia fiunt
talia, tam graviter, si quando poetica surgit
tempestas.[46]

[46] Juv. *Sat.* XII. 22-24.

As Miss Scott points out :

Tales of storms at sea and of shipwreck were common in epic, so common in fact as to be almost a stock epic theme. Both the Odyssey and the Aeneid have elaborate descriptions of storms in which the hero narrowly escapes death, and the same theme recurs in several of the later epics. It is natural therefore that Juvenal should make of his story of Catullus's shipwreck a miniature epic of his own, patterned in general upon the familiar epic tales ; and it is to be expected that Juvenal's parody of this stock theme of epic should show both actual imitations from epic and a free use of epic devices of style.[47]

After illustrating Juvenal's imitation of epics and his employment of epic style, Miss Scott shows Juvenal's novel additions in his exciting account of a fire on shipboard in the middle of the storm and his description of the famous harbor at Ostia at which Catullus' ship finally arrived. The celebration of Catullus' safe return makes the prologue and epilogue to Juvenal's story and their spirit of joy is a happy contrast to the picture of the dangers of the storm. The actual narrative of the tempest occupies only fifty-five lines of the hundred and thirty of the poem so that Juvenal's narrative is less garrulous than the stories of their perils which he says the sailors told after they landed. In spite of its being a parody, Juvenal's tale is a highly successful miniature epic.

Satire XV, his third epic anecdote, has a far more gruesome theme. It is an account of a fight in upper Egypt between the towns of Ombi and Tentyra (Dendyra) and the cannibalism that followed the battle. Editors long believed that Ombi was the modern Kom-Ombo which is a hundred miles from Dendyra so that the two towns could hardly be called neighbors as Juvenal dubbed them. But in 1895 Flinders Petrie discovered remains of another Ombi only ten miles from Dendyra which corresponds to

47 Inez G. Scott, *op. cit.,* p. 83.

Juvenal's description and gives support to his statement that he himself had been in Egypt.[48]   This newly discovered evidence of Juvenal's historicity gives special point to his comparison of himself to Ulysses who, when he told such a tale to Alcinous at the dinner-table, moved some of his hearers to wrath, some to laughter, for they thought him a lying story-teller.   Ulysses was, however, telling of his own adventures.   Juvenal is going to relate a true story that happened lately in the consulship of Juncus.

Juvenal shows his awareness of his epic parody not only by comparing himself as narrator to Ulysses, but by comparing the Egyptian combatants with the famous warriors in Homer's Iliad.   In actual epic imitation, however, Juvenal is closer to Vergil than Homer and seems to follow the structure of the battle between the Trojans and the Latins.[49]   But nothing in Homer or Vergil seems to me to equal the ferocious realism of the meal which the victorious Ombites made off the raw flesh of their fallen foes. Juvenal himself was so fully aware of his culminating horrors that he ends with the emotion which the compassionate Pythagoras would have felt had he lived to see these monstrosities of today.   Also he makes the epilogue to the battle his famous and beautiful passage on pity which begins :

Nature, which gave man tears, proclaims that she gave the human race tender hearts.

This deliberate study of Juvenal's use of anecdotes in his Satires has revealed much about the satirist.   Against a background of his times and a hypothetical reconstruction of his life, his education has been described from his own declarations about its merits, its failures, its gaps and we have seen his reverence for two great teachers, Socrates

[48] Juv. *Sat.* XV. 33–35, 45; Gilbert   [49] Inez G. Scott, *op. cit.,* p. 88.
Highet, *op. cit.,* p. 487.

from whom he learned in spirit, Quintilian whom he may have known.

In the prologue to his Satires, he has given the reasons for his selection of his particular genre of writing, and has described his models, his training, his subjects, his style, his purpose.   From the Satires themselves we have seen that very few of his anecdotes are drawn from mythology ; several are historical ; but the majority are stories from contemporary life.   His method of narration is varied, for he recaptures anecdotes by mere allusion, or he accumulates them in significant lists in which suggested stories are interspersed among rhetorical pictures.   At other times he draws his characters in long sketches with some dialogue and much rhetoric.   Several Satires are integrally anecdotes and these are told deliberately as epic parodies. Through all these varied methods one conscious purpose runs, the moral teaching of a reactionary to a corrupt world.

Juvenal's use of anecdotes is proved by his own words to be the conscious process of a literary artist.   He selects his subjects with discrimination, rejecting time-worn myths for true stories of everyday life in his own times.   He sees that the distinction between satire and epic rests on subject matter rather than on style.   So while discarding the mythological themes of epic, he adopts a grand style that is composed of the epic and the rhetorical.

Every Satire betrays the *rhetor*, for he is a master of the rhetorical oratory which he learned in the schools and which, perhaps, he himself practised.   Quintilian or his kind taught him indeed the use of his moral *sententiae* and his *acria exempla*.   And his satire employs all the familiar rhetorical devices of imagery, amplification, interrogations, apostrophe, direct address, dialogue, hyperbole.

With this rhetorical coloring there is a vast use of epic

diction and epic narration. He imitated epic style for humorous effects in devices of anticlimax, caricature, irony, assumed simplicity, and in prolonged parodies which constitute whole Satires. He also used epic style for serious effects in poetic descriptions and occasional myths. So interwoven are the rhetorical and the epic elements in his Satires that it is hard to decide whether Horace would have called him more of a *rhetor* or a *poeta*.

His writings afford a striking illustration of the contrast between his grandeur and Horace's simplicity, the grand style of his *acria exempla* and the plain style of Horace's *sermones*. Juvenal is consistently and primarily a preacher. Horace is a conversationalist and a Socratic.

Juvenal is not as good a story-teller as a painter of pictures. He often uses what Duff calls an "effective semi-dramatic method in a series of brief scenes." [50] His detailed realism packs each canvas with figures. His intense feeling demands lurid colors. His anecdotes are pictorial and each conveys a message.

This is not disparagement. Juvenal fell on evil days. Life bore hard on him. Out of fear, disappointment and horror, he rose to heights of denunciation and acrimony that isolated him in lonely grandeur. His bread was bitterness for like the Homeric heroes he was gnawing his own heart.

[50] J. Wight Duff, *A Literary History of Rome in the Silver Age,* p. 614.

IX

RETROSPECT

AT the conclusion of my fourth book of studies in Roman fiction,[1] I wish to say a word about their order and relation. I have thought at times that it would have been better if fate, in the form of an invitation to contribute a volume on Apuleius to the series "Our Debt to Greece and Rome," had not ordained that I should write first a book on the one complete novel extant in Latin literature. This is not, however, my present opinion, for out of the study of that famous picaresque novel I was led to consider many precursors, many diverse elements that had converged to create so great a work of art in the realm of fiction : stories from far eastern lands, the beginnings of the Greek novel, romances finding expression in elegiac poems, fictitious cases used as practice training in the rhetorical schools, satire written in prose and verse (the Menippean type) which culminated in a realistic novel, now only a fragment, the *Satyricon*.

And by means of these vari-colored threads which I traced backward one by one as in a labyrinth, I came to a central truth : that the essence of the Latin genius for story-telling lay not in the long novel, but in the short story, for in the last analysis the *Satyricon* appears thor-

[1] *Apuleius and his Influence,* New York, 1937. *Romance in the Latin Elegiac Poets,* New York, 1932. *Essays on Ancient Fiction,* New York, 1936.

oughly episodical and Apuleius' *Metamorphoses* is composed of a tandem of stories held in line by the thin plot of the transformation of a man into an ass and his adventures.

Then I saw that the embryo of the short story is the anecdote, and that the anecdote is a symbol of the Latin psyche, alert to sense impressions, interested in the concrete experience and the individual person, capable of understanding all the world through the little primrose in the crannied wall. Therefore the *exemplum,* the memorable telling of a particular saying or deed, had in Latin literature extended the art of narration to a far wider scope than that of recognized fiction, was indeed an art form in itself, was so recognized by ancient critics and from constant use by genius had become a polished gem of many facets, flashing color and light. So after I saw the significance of these art miniatures, I was led to a detailed study of them in types of writing where their use had been most notable. And after long deliberation I selected as the authors most significant for their handling of them Cicero, Livy, and the Roman satirists.

It may seem strange that I have not included Valerius Maximus' collection of anecdotes in these essays. But his "repertory for speakers" is a mere assemblage of useful anecdotes related in the plainest style and arranged under various classifications. It is not valuable for one who is interested in analyzing the use of anecdotes as a form of art. Moreover, J. Wight Duff has already done full justice to Valerius' *farrago.*[2]

In these separate studies, the inherent value of the anecdote as an art form has emerged. The theories of its origins with the Greek rhetoricians and philosophers, have been traced. Its value has been estimated from

[2] J. Wight Duff, *op. cit.,* pp. 433–51.

Cicero's handling of it, since he as critic and writer, both presented the theory of the *exemplum* and manifested its use in as different types of literature as the oration, the philosophical dialogue and the moral epistle.   Moreover it was Cicero too who developed its embryo to the full-grown, virile *narratio* of great oratory.

Next the whole ancient theory of writing history as moral instruction for individuals and states was demonstrated in Livy's construction of his *Libri ab Urbe Condita* from portentous *exempla*.   In magnificent pageantry centuries of Roman life were portrayed by him in stories of religion, of society, of politics and of war.   Like Cicero, Livy was an artist in the handling of his material, varying the form from brief anecdotes to long, short stories and to inset monographs.   These he colored by as passionate an emotion as inflamed Cicero's oratory.   And in them he expressed great verities by fictitious conversation and speeches which his imagination created as true in spirit though they were not vouched for by records.   Here a great patriot and moralist employed fiction as history and varied his style according to his story.

The satirists, akin as they were to the philosopher-preachers (the Cynics, the Stoics, the Epicureans), found the anecdote an inevitable medium for conveying their moral lessons.   Horace gave it its most genial and conversational tone.   Many of his famous stories might be chats on promenades like those on the streets of Rome with his father, or after-dinner stories like the one told at the Sabine farm by Cervius about the country mouse and the city mouse.   Horace's technique develops from incidental conversation to complete dialogue, which even includes the long diatribe.   In his most elaborate diatribe he shows himself a skillful master of the use of the anecdote for philosophical instruction. In the Epistles, geniality prevails and friend writes to friend in the intimacy of the letter some very human stories.

Persius maintained the traditions for satire handed down by Lucilius and Horace in adopting the hexameter for his form, in imitating the frank fearlessness of the old Attic Comedy and in writing autobiographical anecdotes. His typical stories are philosophical, imbued with his ardent Stoicism. The passion of his faith overrides the cramped character of an immature style which is a mosaic of phrases from Horace, everyday colloquialisms and the language of the rhetorical and the philosophical schools.

Juvenal transformed the plain style of Horace's *sermones* to the grand style suited to his fiery indignation at the wrongs of mankind and to his *acria exempla*. A thwarted life whetted his sword-blade. The impetuosity of his passion made him often rush on in a stream of suggested stories and plunged him into a realism that made his narrative pictorial. His indignation so possessed him that his style had to become heroic. Yet with his eyes on the present, he had no time for the mythology of the past. Intense passion made him arraign mankind before the bar of civilization and pronounce a judge's sentence on the lost cause of human dignity. Yet he was not without the *lacrimae rerum* of pity and he offered for salvation a constructive ideal in his *mens sana in corpore sano*.

Phaedrus and Martial are to be classed in spirit with the satirists though the forms of their short poems set them off as fabulist and epigrammatist. Phaedrus, the freedman of Augustus, made the anecdotal fable the expression of the *vox populi*, an instrument to sound the wrongs of the weak, the oppressed and the slaves. But not content with speaking for his class or with preaching against cupidity and meanness, he sometimes made his anecdotes simple diversions for a sorry world.

Martial like Phaedrus made the small anecdote a separate art form by using it as an epigram. In his poems he illustrates his own theory of writing, for he kept within the traditions of Greek and Roman epigram, yet made the genre peculiarly his own by discarding mythology for reality and by holding the mirror up to nature, or, let us say, by taking moving pictures of all the daily life of the Roman world. The pigments with which he colored his photographs were frankness, wit, humor and occasional tenderness.

Through the studies of these seven authors it has become clear that each was an artist with definite theories about his own technique and sensitive awareness of the processes by which he achieved his style. In each, critical and creative genius working together as whetstone for the sharpening of the tools and as the tools themselves (file, rapier, and stylus) produced the peculiar *color* which Horace demanded from every poem. So the anecdote, though a miniature in dimensions, came to have its recognized and fitting place in literary art in as widely different fields as the philosophical dialogue, the moral epistle, the oration, history, satire, fable, and epigram.

INDEX

A

Academy, school of philosophy, 91
Accius, 121
Achilles, 25, 162
Addison, J., 131
Aebutia, 64
Aebutius, Publius, 63, 64, 65
Aemilia, wife of Scipio Africanus, 60
Aeneas, 162
Aeneid, 173
Aesop, 5, 6, 95, 96, 97, 98, 99, 101, 104, 105, 108, 109, 110, 113
Aesopian, 85, 98
Aesopus, an actor of Cicero's time, 82, 93
Agamemnon, 19, 91
Agave, 91
Agrippa, 90
Agrippa, Menenius, 6, 40
Ajax, 91
Albinus, Lucius, 55
Alcibiades, 143, 150, 151
Alcinous, 162, 174
Alexander, the Great, 14, 25, 76, 77, 165
Alfius, the money-lender, 94
Amphion, 168
Amphitheater, Flavian, 121
Anacharsis, 13, 96
Anecdotes (*exempla*), art of writing, sources, 1
   definitions of terms, 2-6
   training in use of, 6-7
   narratio, 7-8
   story-teller and audience, 8-9
   in Cicero, Livy and the satirists, *passim*
Antiochus, 25, 32, 59
Antisthenes, 3
Antony, 25
Apollinaris, 126
Apollo, 100, 167, 168
Apollonius, of Panhormus, 33

A (continued)

Apologue, 2, 5
Apophthegm, 2, 4, 5
Apuleius, 177, 178
Aquinum, 158
Aratulla, 133
Archimedes, 16
Ardea, 57
Aricia, 172
Aristides, 20
Aristippus, 3, 82, 84, 91
Aristophanes, 148
Aristotle, 3
Arria, 128, 129, 138, 141, 142
Astapa, in Spain, 75
Asturicus, 169
Atellan farces, 86
Athens, 113, 159, 160
Auctor ad Herennium, 1, 4, 7, 8
Aulus Gellius, 95
Aulus Postumius, 67
Avianus, 95
Avidienus, 83
Augustine, 155

B

Bacchae, of Euripides, 84
Bacchanalian conspiracy, 51, 62-66
Bacchus, 51, 63, 64, 131, 132
Bassus, 134, 135
Bellerophon, 166
Bellona, 49
Bilbilis, 120, 138
Biton, 15
Bowdoin College, vii
Britain, 126
Broadway Translations, vii, 123
Bruegel, Pieter the Elder, 169
Brutianus, 121
Brutus, 18, 47, 67
Buecheler, F., 171
Butler, H. E., 78